BECOME A KING

OR

REMAIN A PAWN

Andy Hertz

YOU WERE BORN TO WIN, NOT TO FEEL SORRY FOR YOURSELF!

ANDY HERTZ

ISBN: 9798646142598

*Thank you to all those who believed in me and
offered me support in difficult times.*

*Thanks to those who are building a better
world, no matter where they are
and what their social status is
or what they have received from life.*

*Thank you for choosing to read these lines.
And especially to my mother,
because she gave me life!*

ANDY HERTZ

PROLOGUE

IT IS WITH ENTHUSIASM that I've written the book *Become a King or Remain a Pawn*, to share my passion and knowledge for business. I strongly believe that it is integral that we learn to handle money. The reality is that most of us did not get direction in that matter, not as children, nor later. If you look around, the world is full of poor accountants or employees of banks who are dependent on they work, people who handle money. However, many still remain at the stage of „pawns". In this book you will find only a very few description of digits. A business must be created with passion. For a business to thrive, it requires dedication, work, lifelong learning, self-determination, establishment of relationships, courage, quality marketing, ideas, practice, and finding and using opportunities. The way this is brought about must follow a well-chosen way for the soul, and reflect your wishes and possibilities. The beginning of the road will require greater effort so that you may enjoy thereafter life, family, freedom and everything else you want. So if you get to live out of inertia, at least to be the inertia of a well-done thing, of a life full of abundance. Money does not have to be a goal, but rather a tool, an element that will help you to free yourself from the chains of the system that exploits you from the moment you set your alarm clock for your first day of work. When you get caught in this system, it can make you sell your time, give up pleasures and, in some cases, make you stray from the road that you really want to travel throughout your life. Moreover, it makes you lose direction from other possibilities and sets you in one direction, losing sight of your dreams. Most people accept this system as an inheritance; they adopt from their parents the belief that this is the only way to live. Most will remain faithful to these beliefs for their entire life, even educating their children in the same way. And the others, few and free, will lead them!

This book will help you become aware of your situation so that you may start a new road, to create, to take responsibility for your life and what happens around you, to find the way to free yourself from the circle of "pawns," that you may find yourself in. You will also find business ideas here, positive and negative experiences of my life, some various solutions, impressions of different areas of work, something about goals and vision, and about taking action, all seen through my eyes.

If you have not read my first book *Life, The Best Birthday Gift*, I describe living in more than five places so far, starting from a wonderful place called Săvârşin, Arad County, until presently (2015), living in Southwark, London, UK. Every place taught me something and informed different aspects of my life.

This book is written for every human being open to change and responsibility to make that change. I have written it in such a way that if I were to go back in time, I wish I could find this book there, to be sure it would help me. If I had found this book a long time ago, written by someone else, it would have been very good...

I hope it will help you!

ANDY HERTZ

<u>INTRODUCTION</u>

WHAT ARE YOU DOING WITH YOUR LIFE?

SOME HAVE STARTED the road of life on higher ground, others from the path below. Not all of us have been born into a rich family, not all of us were exempt from shortcomings. Even though I grew up in a quiet and beautiful environment, in which I was well educated, I did not necessarily have financial education. Some of us may have poor parents, maybe some not have them at all, or maybe some we have not learned the right lessons from them, or other lessons related to financial education. Or their teachings do not help us escape from the vicious circle in which we fell without our will, a circle in which, before, they probably fell also. And without financial education, we cannot leave the road upon which we were set during our childhood. Money does not bring happiness, but lack thereof inhibits experience, clean and healthy food, and the ability to provide children with necessary skills. It will prevent us from finding our freedom and tranquility, a fulfilled and peaceful life. Sure, a good car does not necessitate that you will live happily. But with an old one, you will waste your time on various expenses - mechanics, month by month, will eat at your nerves.

I have already written in *Life, The Best Birthday Gift* about health, friends, passions and some business ideas. In this book, I decided to write about career, money and business, because, in their absence, you cannot truly enjoy life. Therefore, I think money is of major importance in personal development.

> *Let him who would move the world,*
> *first move himself.*
>
> *Socrates*

Why *Become a King or Remain a Pawn*? From the title, you can understand that I will talk about a radical change and, at the same time, I will try to explain what it means to stay in a state of inertia. To do so, in careers there exist "kings" and "pawns". Leaders and subordinates. Independent people and dependent people. Whether you are in the first category or the second, whether you are the king or the pawn, you are part of the same board game, namely, life. If you are open to change, you must do so realistically. Reading this book means you are willing to make a change, perhaps for the first time consciously. You have been in this game for a long time, and to enact change, you must expect it to come from within you. When you are stuck in the position of a pawn, if you wait passively for the change, it will not come: if you want something to change in the future, you must make a change now.

Why either a king or pawn? Because, nowadays, you do not have to be a king in order to live like a king. Nowadays, you live the way you choose to live. The pawn, however, will remain living a humble life, doing nothing special. Remaining dependent upon a state of continuous relaxation, you will encounter those more determined to exceed their limits and pursue their dreams, and it will pass you by. If you love your job, however, and you do not want anything more, if you do not have the courage to take life in your own hands and put in a little more effort, if you do not like being independent, or if you have already chosen a good direction for your career, then this book is not addressing you. But I have to take the possibility to remain a pawn.

As I said in my first book, I do not think there can be happiness for those who cannot afford to buy children's clothes or pay the current bill. Money is necessary in any place at any step. That is, if you do not choose to live a rough life like a hermit in a cave. Money does not change man, although many believe this and all kinds of myths about money, invented by the poor, because in many places is needed an excuse or reason for poverty. Just being good man, with money or without money, you will remain the same: good. Or, if you get vile with money, why do not you become vile without money? It's a boundless stupidity to believe that money brings evil into your life. A bad man - envious and gullible, of course, will amplify these attributes with the growth of his wealth. There is no greater a mistake for a man to make than to desire solely money. Money, quite simply, is paper. We can choose what we do with money - multiply it, or distribute it. When you give up your life to sell your time, energy, and health simply to make more money, after which you will spend it things which you do not need, you make the biggest possible mistake in the world. Your time is short, that's why you must look to make money through a good plan, and with passion and fun. It must be according to your own choices, so that you will have time for family, for rest and for everything you still want to do outside of your career. Build your dream, nothing else, and with that, enough money will come. Do not track its gain, but rather your plan for a beautiful and fulfilled life, and the fun you have along the way. If you do not have a plan or an idea or you do not know how to start, this book might be important for you. I write it for you, with love, thoughts, ideas and plans accrued through the experience that has brought me to the point where I am at now. Come on, let's travel together for a while, and you will find your way of fulfillment. It is enough for all to have.

Maybe you really have enough money, you have a good car, a house big enough for you and your family, you allow a wonderful holiday every year and you have a happy family. From the outside, it appears very good. But there is one thing that does not fit into our little jigsaw puzzle: Monday. If Mondays ruin your mood on Sunday, and even the next few days, you are not where you need to be. How many working days are there in thirty five years of work, and how many free days do you recall?

What about your soul? What about the mornings that you would like to be a little lazy, then drink your coffee, but instead you have to run through the rain and cold to work? What about the plans that you have dreamed of for years, where do they fit in?

This world offers us so much - why do we not

feel free to choose anything? Why do we limit ourselves with the outdated ideology that we have to accept what has been given to us, that we should not risk anything, and that we have to follow the path of others and find a safe job? I think that Monday must be equal to all other days of the week and must be the way that you choose it to be, not others, because it is, after all, your life. So that you may make Mondays not be a burden, you have to find solutions to do what you like. That's why you must become rich. Rich does not mean the one who has a lot of money, but rather the one who makes money, being, at the same time, happy day to day. Rich is the one who enjoys to the fullest the road he has chosen for his life.

If you love fishing and hate going to work, then transform your fishing, your passion, into your life. You need money to live; however, a safe job that only brings in money will not necessarily bring a happy family. Find that activity, that beautiful passion that allows you to make money. It's true: not all of this will happen overnight, but we'll talk about it a little later. And yes, for many, there may not be a way to develop a business or to make some intelligent investments to generate profit.

How many times have you asked yourself what you're looking for on the Earth? Were you born to work to death, from one month to the next, limited and enclosed in a cage in which you lie yourself? Or you were born to leave something great behind, to lead a prosperous life, to give your children everything they will need, to enjoy every day of the week? Nothing is more desirable than to jump out of bed every morning, full of energy, for a new day that you look forward to. And the time spent in the midst of your loved ones must not be limited by psychologically tiring activities. What about those who went abroad, focused on money, and who did not see their children grow up?

So that you may enjoy every day, so you can enjoy your spare time and fulfill your dreams, you need good health. You cannot be healthy when you are always sad, tired, and unhappy, without a will. Everything connects somewhere at some point. To be well, every day must be yours. If you wake up in the morning and go to the work not in a good mood, without a will, without appetite, unhappy ...one day the chain will break. You cannot walk endlessly on a journey through the mud. Your feet start to sink. Eventually, you will tire and fall, and looking behind you, you will see nothing. Some say that they make sacrifices for their children. The problem is this: your children are following your example. It is difficult to tell them not to smoke while you light the cigarette in your hand. How can you create, and give all to your children and to the world, when you lack energy and your soul is drowned in the muddy lake of unhappiness?

> *For the love of money is the root of the evil.*
>
> *1 Timothy 6:10*

Not money should be your goal, but the happiness of doing what you want to do. The money and the reward will come surely. God will rejoice and reward you when he sees that you are properly living your life - you live joyfully, giving the world everything that you can. Money, in itself, is not evil, but the love of money becomes a disease.

If you ask the children of wealthy people if they want to be remain rich, they will answer that they do not need money, but instead they need quality time with their parents. Once they grow up, they realize that without money they cannot do much around. Cannot help others, cannot create much and cannot enjoy life in all aspects.

The poor, however, believe that being rich means taking holidays in the Maldives, Tenerife and Bali. Well, from my experience, being rich means a lot of work. Very few who play the lottery will win. Very few, also, become rich through inheritance. All the others make money through work. Even some who have received inheritances, still through work they maintain their wealth.

If you want to be rich, set your hands to work and your mind to learn, and later, you will also find your free time. The biggest gain you will see will be the work done with pleasure and independence.

I will now tell you the story of a Romanian businessman who started with nothing. He lived in a poor town where opportunities and potential were lacking. When the factories closed, he took his wife to work abroad. There, he worked as a plumber, and she cleaned people's homes. They gathered money for a few years, after which they returned to their city as poor as they had left it. They lived in a two-room apartment they had bought with their wedding money, many years before. They invested all the money made abroad in a prosperous business at the time - a window blinds company. Everyone was putting window blinds in their offices and houses, throughout the villages. They gathered a reasonable sum, and when the industry seemed to be drying up, they opened a new firm dealing with the installation of thermal/gas boilers - this was the prosperous industry at the moment. Soon, they upsized into other cities and expanded the services they offered to their customers: they formed maintenance teams and revisions, gas checks, troubleshooting. But their office remained in one modest apartment. Only after investing money in assets (commercial premises, apartments and land), they built impressive headquarters and a large deposit. When they had

17

finally made a lot of money, they were completely free to dream and to relax. Today, they have a successful company with offices in many cities, and many properties that provides income through real estate without the need to work. If the money earned abroad would have been spent on the house they had dreamed of before, they would have nothing left for business or for investment, today, they would have been simple laborers living from one month to the next. Now, they can always leave work and money will come for them from the investments made in a wise way.

People go to work, it's normal. But if you get out of this circle, will be enough drivers anyway for the buses or factory workers. Not many people realize what they can do with their life. After realizing this myself, I thought that it would be hugely difficult for me to accept a job that many desire. However, I chose freedom instead of being a factory manager, I chose to walk through the mountains, instead of being crowded on the bus on my way to work, and I chose to love Monday!

CHAPTER 1

THE FIRST STEPS

I'LL BEGIN WITH the part you may not want to hear, so that I'm preparing you.

Reasons why to stay as a pawn and not do business:

- There is more stress, sometimes.
- You will have more responsibility on your shoulders.
- Maybe business is not what you really want.
- You make decisions for others; not others for you.

- Initially, you will work longer and free time will decrease, until your business starts working for you.
- In business there are risks - if you do not want to take them, this way of life is not for you.
- Many new firms go bankrupt within the first five years.

Now, why choose to do business? Why should you become a king? Why should you choose to develop your dream?

- You are your own boss.
- You do what you choose to do.
- You are more flexible when it comes to waking up in the morning.
- You can be creative.
- It can be greatly profitable.
- You can help others.
- You can work from home.
- You can determine your time as you like.
- You can leave as an inheritance what you create.
- No one can fire you.
- You will become more determined.
- You can become financially independent.
- You can create jobs.
- You will be challenged.
- You will surround yourself with the people you choose.
- You will learn a lot.

- You will spend every day in the setting chosen by you.
- You can fulfill your dreams.

As spent my days navigating London's massive metro stations at peak hours, I saw hundreds and thousands of people breathing on each other's backs as they took tiny steps towards the escalators. I hope not to offend, but I can't not to associate that mass of people with a flock of sheep being directed against their will. I can swear that 99% of them would like to be elsewhere in those moments rather than on their way to their workplaces. If it happens that you pass through this daily, one of the first steps is to realize that you are on the wrong path. The second is to choose to leave, and to embark on a new one, chosen this time by you. But not today! You first have to create a smart and achievable plan. Like in chess game, you need thinking time and strategy. You must think of other possible moves before you make your decision.

Your task is not to seek for love, but merely to seek and find all the barriers within yourself that you have built against it.

Rumi

Now, see the statement above through the success in business or career, in general. Your goal is not to look directly for success, but to remove the barriers that you may have put up between yourself and success. Let's take me, as an example: those who know me, they are familiar with my achievements, as with a bodybuilder you see daily and you do not realize how much he grew, until you compare it to the beginning of the endeavor. Well, I remember, not many years ago, I had nothing but a "safe" job. Now, although I'm still on the road, I already own real estate which brings me monthly income, I have a good plan on that I follow, and I am peace. But I'm still on my way. In the book "Life, the Best Birthday Gift" I set out the concrete elements of the plan I'm following, relating specifically to my experience with real estate.

A few steps for following the road of success:

- You must have a plan.
- You must spend time with people doing what you want to do. You will learn much from them, and they will provide support.
- People who only think about money and do not experience the pleasures of starting a business do not have a very high chance of success. If you ask them how much money they ultimately want, they will have no idea.
- Work efficiently.
- Trust in yourself.
- Know your purpose.

- Do not listen to the advice of those who are inexperienced or uninterested. Learn from professionals.
- Give yourself time to study your chosen domain. Read books and educate yourself financially. You must endeavor to do this yourself - schools do not teach you how to make money.
- Focus on saving to be able to start a business, and then make as much money as you want.
- Take advantage of opportunities after you learn to find them.
- Use money wisely and save part of them.
- Do not become greedy and never forget to help those in need.
- Every step must be judged right, in this period when you can buy illusions.
- Learn to stop when is needed and do not subject your business to a high risk.

Simply deciding that you can do whatever you want is the easy part; but putting this proposition into action is more difficult. The action is born through the question -*How can I do this?* This puts in motion the thought processes of determining what you can do with action, and, if you do not act, what opportunities you will miss out on.

Giving up on what you do wrong, or on what you not love or enjoy, does not mean that you must stop or reverse the course of your life, but rather that,

23

from that point, you begin on a new road that represents the chance to do something truly great.

If you desire to change, it should come not because of others, but for your soul.

The journey of a thousand miles begins with a single step.

Chinese proverb

We'll all leave a story behind us. You can choose how great your story will be. I choose that my story does not remain mediocre. What do you choose?

CHAPTER 2

GET OUT OF YOUR COMFORT ZONE

Why should I stay at the bottom of a well,
when a strong rope is in my hand?

Rumi

IF YOU THINK THAT your parents are living a poor life, and you do not want to follow their path, learn that you can reach their age in even more difficult circumstances - being much more unhappy, alone or with someone with you do not share to many memories and love, but rather on a basis of needs and troubles to be resolved. So I'm telling you to look out of as many angles you can to

25

the living in two, a marriage relationship or coexistence. „Up to an age you choose, after an age you gather", say the elders. This also applies to business. If you think your parents have a poor life, and you do not want to follow them, you obviously must choose another way than theirs. I strongly believe that if I did it, you can do it too. If I grew up without help or resources and I managed to get here by myself, then so you can do it too!

If you spend most of your time in your comfort zone, it means that you have given up using everything at its full potential. You have to do everything you can to live a full life. I am aware that I am responsible for my future in business. It's up to me to learn, to inform myself, to look for the right people, to be in the right places. Success will not come to me if I stay at home. Potential business partners or customers will not come get me out of bed. I have to look for them.

> *And in the end, it's not the years in your life that count. It's the life in your years."*
>
> *Abraham Lincoln*

Man lives on average no more than 960 months. The first and last 20 years of life I will not count for work. That means for work are left about 480 months. If you are very young, you have 480 months left for work. If you are about 30 years old, you have about 360 months left for work. If you have 40 years, you've got about 240 months for work. What do you choose to do with them? How will you spend this time? There is better use than, in the next 10 to 30 months, to create a plan. Is it not better to take time to learn about a new career or business, and to afterwards spend your life as you want, than to spend it entirely the way you do not want it?

Do not expect a tragedy to be forced to change your life. Change your life because you want it to be better, not because you want to avoid poverty or hunger. Try not to get to a point where this is the case. And if you have gotten yourself there, that's all the reason you need to start something new.

In hard times, you must break from your routine, out of your comfort zone. In the worst case, you do not want it, and it is forced upon you. In the best case, you do it willingly. When it happens, you learn; stretching your limbs, pushing your body with the power of the one who has nothing to lose, you build resistance to challenges and you rise and descend without regret and without fear.

Why did I leave my comfort zone? Honestly, have forgotten what it is like to live within it, to live essentially for nothing. I do not remember anymore the last time I've spent my entire day from morning

27

to night watching TV. Currently, I really like to be active in, most importantly, the real estate in which I've successfully invested in recent years, I like to do my writing. When get some free time, I write. I know electrical systems and electronics, after graduating from two schools in the field. Before I left for the UK, I developed a jewelry business, where I learned how to make, import and sell them. I know the value of people in business related areas. And I trust that if I want, I can set up, starting from nothing, almost any type of business. I know the laws and the operation of the banking system. All of this, I learned myself. After I had 150 subordinates, I can say that I'm good at managing things. And, most importantly, I learned to look for and find helpful information when I need it. What I do now every day is that which matters most to me, and I have fun doing things.

Many years ago, I could hardly wait to leave work, to come home and sit in front of the television or other leisure activities. Now, looking back, I realize that those years were devoid of anything memorable, and I did not live - I merely existed.

Positive thinking must be followed by action. Positive thinking will take you out of your comfort zone. If you see yourself in the future as a prosperous businessman and you believe that you can become as you dream, you will start looking for solutions. Over time, you will realize that your dreams fade or even disappear, the longer you stay not doing much of anything. If you see yourself as poor, so you will stay. If you see yourself as rich, you will act, because you have set your direction and made up your mind.

I'm sure that in every man's life will come the moment where he will look back and regret that he did not done some things at the right time. At that time it will likely be late to realize and live old dreams. Looking back to the past, you realize that you lacked courage, you did not took risks, but you did things as others wanted, you felt bound to things and you lost people dear to you, you did not change anyone's life for the better, you did not realize anything you wanted, really, and you are only a reflection of the man you could have become.

If you stay in your comfort zone, you can lose sight of your own personality, and even lose people around you who have great aspirations. In this way, some have had their life transformed into a sort of hell.

Give light,
and the darkness will disappear of itself.

Erasmus

Advice for leaving your comfort zone and routine:

- Make a plan. Write it down, and keep it in a place that you will see it every day.
- Trust yourself. Start with small steps, but do one every day.
- Read something about the fields that you will immerse yourself in.
- Do sports following a clear plan. You'll be healthier and you will learn discipline.
- Seek new activities that give you pleasure; they will help you to „wake up", embracing change.
- Give up bad or/and unnecessary habits.
- Meet new people, preferably who share your passions.
- Be honest with yourself.
- Do not make excuses; assume your past actions, and especially those that will come.
- Write down the benefits of leaving the comfort zone.
- Educate yourself through school or course in an area that will help you find your way again.
- Cherish your time.
- Focus on fun and passion.
- Set your targets so as to overcome your „old" limits.
- Find ways to self-motivate.
- Use the time you have left. The only real failure is when you give up before you begin. Give up your fear and start living!

BECOME A KING OR REMAIN A PAWN

ANDY HERTZ

CHAPTER 3

WHAT TO GIVE UP

I RECOMMEND YOU to give up on what is not good for you, to what you do not love, to what does not help you to grow, so you can build your life dream of. Free yourself from bad to make room for the good. With iron balls shackled to your feet, it's hard to conquer a mountain. Cut them off and let them fall downhill and you can climb faster enjoying the road, if you really want to climb the mountain. What exactly do these iron balls represent? They are the people who pull you down, negative thoughts, fear, selfishness, lack of education...

It is said that you are the media of a few people who are day by day around you. I hope that you stick with beautiful people, who are going up the mountain. If not, give up to the environment that won't let you climb. This is very important! Drop down the people who drag you down. Most of them are so unhappy that they almost feel guilty for being born, or worse, wish to never have been born. They view life as torturous and they necessarily want to convince you of their reality. Run away from them! Run back to your life, back to your world! And from there try to help them. People often have different opinions from yours and they do not wish the best for your success. They are either jealous or want to have confirmation that their way of life in which they feel comfortable is good, and cannot accept that you will succeed in a world where they do not have the courage to step.

Sometimes you have to learn to say „No". I know people with a beautiful soul, and others use them, using their goodness. If they are too sensitive, or even kind, they do not know to say „No". If you are in this situation, test those who always ask you for help and see if they are willing to reciprocate. This does not mean it must come down to your personal interests over others, and selfishness, but you must learn what to give up on; you shouldn't waste energy and time. This kind of people are those who really are not worth your effort.

Give up to mourn for mercy and take life as how you receive it. Discover and learn about more options, more ways of life. Do not be satisfied with only what you have, thinking that this is the only path for you. You will learn that there are always more options and ways, and you will see that there in the world is always something for everyone. As there is no wild animal who cannot find his needed for his life, so there is no man who does not find the necessary things for his life. But as a wild animal the man must seek around.

Give up the believing that the time is never now. Now is the right time to reflect on your whole life and the rest of your life start right now. Begin right now to build memorable your life.

Give up the myth which says that rich people thieves and the poor are honest and happy.

Give up doing things done just to impress others. Do not do things for show. They will cost your money, time, energy and many others, and, eventually, you'll see that you haven't enriched your life by doing them.

Give up fears that hold you back. Start with awareness. Generally, you focus on what you want in a positive way or you focus on your fears? Almost all of your fears will not come true, especially if you don't think about them. The negative thoughts can come from all kinds of experiences. When you get to realize them, you learn to ignore them.

Give up expecting something great from the outside. Better think what the best things you ever done, and if you did not to many wonderful things for those around you, do them now.

Once I told to a close relative some personal business plans and I found myself with the following reply:

-Well, you want money to come to you and to be a business owner? He said with superiority and joking.

-Yes! That's exactly what I want! I replied.

-? ? ? ?

He did not expect my response this way.

Some people, especially after a lifetime of working without knowing about business, they cannot believe that some of us can make money by what we choose to do. Give up to absorb knowledge or beliefs of others, even if they share them with a good faith. On your way, no matter what you choose, you'll find many people who will tell you that „it's not good to do what you want do".

A beautiful family, a profitable business, a good school and much more are built with self-work. Those who doesn't like to work have a hellish joy of seeing others low, seeing in the same time they status as acceptable. Do not let them! They will say you cannot climb the rock. They will tell it's hard, you will not get there and you're not good enough. Go up and prove that you can, and many will follow you. Do not do like them, do not let them down.

You want to change the world, you want to have more money, want to develop a business, you want to help others, you want to leave something behind, you want to create, you want to have a life with memorable moments, and then you find all sorts of excuses. You start to say you cannot do it because: you have no help, you were born with no luck, you don't have enough, and you have no relationships, and no ... no ... no ... But in fact, in front of whom do you apologize? What does it matter to others that you will or not have memorable moments, happy days or a thriving business?

Finding all kinds of excuses, you end up not changing the world, not making more money, not developing business, not helping others, not and not... Give up the excuses and their place found reasons for success. Give up excuses for a bad situation, because they will never lead to positive experiences.

When you feel lost, everything goes wrong. When you feel good, all things are going well. Give up negative thoughts and fear. What is, it is. What you cannot change, will remain unchanged anyway. And beyond the clouds of your mind is love, strength, passion, talent. Spread the clouds in your mind and you illuminate every place that you pass through.

Do not worry. Worries often come when you are not well informed. And, always, on what you focus increases.

We live in a world full of victims. Give up or victimize you or not get in the game. You can not change your family you belong or the environment in which you grew up, and you cannot change the gray skies of London. Do what you can do better, where you are, with what you have, and go ahead.

While you chase thieves and lazy ones, weeds are growing in your garden. Give up comparing yourself with others and wasting time to track bad actions of others. If you can not help them, leave them behind.

Give up lazy and meaningless life activities. Give up wasting time in general. Set your priorities, focus on what you want, and learn!

Drop defects and commodity. Start doing sports, you need health.

Give up the belief that you know everything. Accept advice from those you appreciate or from those you choose as mentors, and learn from them.

Give up competing, vanity and childish jealousy. Help others to stand with you. Your most important motivation is must be not to overtake someone, but to be happy and to live each day as you want.

Give up everything that brings you unhappiness. For that what you do and don't brings you happiness, keeps you away from being who you really are. This way you can lose your identity.

Run away from gossip around yourself. It's the most despicable occupation.

Give up mistrust people. Only for you've been through all kinds of events does not mean to live enclosed in a shell. Of all the people around you, very few of them will disappoint you, and, for them, the rest, the majority, not worth your absence trustworthy.

Give up waiting for luck. Luck is about seeking opportunities.

Give up blaming others for your problems. Rather than do that, better looking for solutions to your problems.

In general, focus on the positive things, help others to succeed, create, learn, forgive, respect and love!

And another thing, to go get a serious and healthy way of life, quit grandstanding. Do not throw money around, especially those money you don't really have yet, do not get into debt in order to impress others. Not use your first money or money borrowed from the bank to buy expensive furniture for office, or an extravagant space, luxury cars or who knows what kind of coffee machine. Leave fads for later, when money will come naturally from profits. It is said that your car should reflect up to 10% of your wealth. I would say that the car should reflect that money that came from profit, which you can miss.

Let me tell a short story, a fact. A man of about 45 years old, father and husband, started a construction company with money borrowed from the bank, while economic peak. His business seemed to be prosperous and reached a considerable number of employees, works have started in several areas. Up here, so good. He bought a company headcounters for him and the staff around, had some expensive things for the offices, plus cars, unnecessary expenses, and slowly began to catch up the profits. When the downturn started, around 2008, when he gave up control on his team, ignoring small problems occurred every day, forgetting its vital role in the smooth running of things, after a moment of glory which seemed to never end, instead of investing in assets to generate profits, he ended up with all the goods taken by banks. Even his daughter apartment and the last car they have been taken away. He moved with his family to the country, with his parents. True, the financial crisis had a very big role in this fall. But, that catastrophic bankruptcy could be avoided with a serious, wise and responsible attitude. So try to spend as little, especially in the beginning. If how buy a place for your office, and you have enough space, rent it to others. This way you'll earn money from the rent and you will make extra money by sharing also the maintenance bills.

Ah, I almost forgot something very important! Give up the city and congestion, even occasionally. How many time you can, return to nature! You'll understand why.

And let the expectations of society, friends and family. Live as you want. Be free!

ANDY HERTZ

CHAPTER 4

VALUES, MODELS AND RELATIONSHIPS

VALUES, PRINCIPLES, morals and ethics are related to education.

You can find models everywhere. Successful people are not are hidden in a single place in the world. They are everywhere.

Do not copy and do not compare, especially those which misses. Learn from successful people that are guided by values like those you follow. Thus, you do so that things to happen in your way.

The principles are very important. People who are guided by solid values generally lead to a beautiful life. These values, followed, bring to you more

happiness and life balance. The core values that would be good to watch after are:
- Honesty;
- Confidence;
- Courage;
- Respect;
- Health;
- Family and friends;
- Love.

> 10 Whoever can be trusted with very little can also be trusted with much, and whoever is dishonest with very little will also be dishonest with much.
> 11 So if you have not been trustworthy in handling worldly wealth, who will trust you with true riches?
>
> *Luke 16: 10-11*

Choose your mentors from the people who inspire you or from the most honest ones you know. Do not be impressed by the false greatness of those who achieve success unjustly. They enjoy a false and fleeting success. Many successful companies fallen with a political party or a politician. Your attention should only be channeled to a clean and honest business. In future, after you develop something and move on the path you choose, you will need peace of mind. If you are looking for ways to make money fast and dishonest, you are not reading the right book.

As I said, not all those who seem to be successful is based on some healthy principles, and that success is false and does not take for very long time. In addition, it is highly paid. The existence of some companies was necessary for those who wanted or still want to launder money. How do you think a man who has nothing to do with business, has opened a company that is doing extremely well from the first? What you don't know is that he is there just to filter goods, services and the money come from somewhere above and return almost all in that direction. You have to learn to read if a man's of success is due to himself or others. Why is it good to know that? To avoid being drawn into dangerous games. Remember that rotten apple spoils the good ones.

People, as a model

Avarice of the rich is a misunderstanding. They do not need a penny as currency itself, but value money in general. They have created a way life that the poor do not understand. If you don't look a penny, don't even look at the fact that you have maybe 8 cars in the company, but it needs only 6. You don't look at the fact that employees smoke 20 cigarettes in 8:00

at work, which means an hour lost every day. If you have 10 employees, in this case lose more than 10 hours of work a day. This means that an employee does not work at all, even more than an employee. Of course, I don't think it's good to induce some rules so strict in your company. People must feel good at work. But I want to explain how thinks a man who made money, starting from the bottom. As a "professional defect", he counts each penny and in the end, it results in a huge amount. The rich who spend money without care, they not really made them from scratch. Rather, they inherited them.

As an example, I have seen not once, at supermarket, one man before me, who when receiving the rest, laughed saying: *Leave it so!* or *Keep the change!* From that moment I knew he is a poor man.

So, do not laugh at the rich man who leans after a lost penny that he sees on the street. This is a way of life. The rich man did not get rich because of money found on the floor, but was enriched by this attitude. He bought good products and how cheaper employed people as best payroll not too big, he bought small office space or small buildings that can develop a profitable company and sustainable. If you are „generous" with little money, are „open hand" all the time. Those who develop a profitable business from the bottom up, never throw the money out the window.

It's good to be careful with small money, but pay attention to large and long-term businesses. A manager of over 2000 people told me in time when I was manager over 150 people: *Do not help the workers by helping one, for helping one you lose the rest of them. You have to see the factory as a whole!* That's how it is in business. You have to see the whole picture, not every little detail all the time. That, somehow, not to stay among them forever. Your business must be build such a way that will work without you, if you pursue freedom. Otherwise, you will be the slave of your own invention.

Find winners and follow their principles

Winners always find solutions. Business winners find money for investment, attract people into the game and have fun. And they too, the winners in business, often use other people's money. And they too, the winners, create jobs!

Your actions will be affected by the advice that you listen to. The opinions of those who don't dare to do much great things in life, will always be contrary to what you want to do if you're bold. Some, if you stay in a two-room apartment, will say that you are doing well and that you have everything you want. Others

47

will say that you have not done enough and you don't have enough. If you do not know what you really want, you will listen at random.

Then there are other people who want to impress. That's what happens. They are, generally, people you may admire. But if know them better, you would realize that they are ordinary people and they also have their problems, not necessarily caring about what you are doing. Of course, you can be appreciated, but no one really cares about what you do, except your family and those close to you. So don't put so much value on what you think others will believe about you. It doesn't matter that much.

An unsuccessful man, when he is physically and mentally healthy, generally it has the following characteristics: lazy, ignorant, strong ego, frustrated, boring, ruthless, irresponsible, hasty, and so on. Think of a man that you can choose as a model, as an example to follow in many ways, and find the qualities that you appreciate at him.

Here are some characteristics of the people that I respect and I choose as models: they are enthusiastic, funny, they think before they speak, are sociable, forgiving, innovative, creative, productive and powerful, organized, honest, respectful, responsible, diplomatic, patient, calm, and so on. Now let's see what we lack in order to be the same. If I take each attribute in part, I realize that I lack nothing to be like those whom I appreciate. I can be funny, I can think before I speak, I can be creative, I learned to be strong, I am calm, and so on. You also nothing to be even better than those we admire. Successful people are no more beautiful than unsuccessful people, they are not necessary healthier, they do not live in a particular place, they do not have necessary more talent than those who are not successful. But they do things in a different way.

Whatever model you follow, do not be satisfied to reaching it. Your path is different, and your goal is to be happy. You don't have to reach out to the others or defeat them, but to get where you want, for yourself.

Try to appreciate modest people. Those who do not boast, those who are not arrogant, those who do things for show. They will teach you what you need to know next.

If those around you are poor or unsuccessful, it is obviously wise not to follow their path and they financial advice. I know this call sounds rather weird or harsh, especially when it comes to loving people, who have the best intentions. However, if you follow their path, it will take you where they are. The poor are usually firmly convinced that money attracts evil and that money are very difficult to be achieved, and that without luck you cannot achieve success. They also believe that without money you cannot make money or that if you were born poor, you will remain so. At the same time, they are convinced that the amount in your account has to do with the school you have done and the chosen profession, with the national economy or relations, theft and unclean business. I tell you to follow the path or advice of those who do not take stupid risks, who have been successful starting from the bottom, who make as much money as they need, take on responsibilities, always learn, invest, build their life, think about high level and long term, are positive and know how to put the money to work for them.

> *Some people come in our life as blessings.*
> *Some come in our life as lessons.*
>
> *Mother Teresa*

Build connections.

Every person you meet is added to the group of people who can help you or you can help, at one point, and, until then, you're having fun together. How do you make new friends with whom to share the same ideals?

Before the Holidays, I opted for a vegan diet for a while. It is a diet, a lifestyle, which excludes consumption of animal products. It was very interesting. When I walked into the supermarket where I usually shop, to buy vegan diet products for the first time, it seemed like I was walking there for the first time. I discovered many products that I had never seen before, even though they were there all the time. Passion fruit (weird), coconut milk, basil sauce and so on. Leaving that aside, I found another interesting thing. I discovered that there is a whole community of vegans, even restaurants on this topic, online groups. If you want to make friends and new topics for discussion, do new things. Dare and try, especially since you only have to learn from all of this. Maybe, this way, you can even find things that will change your life for the better.

Get into politics. There you will find capable and influential people. There is nothing wrong with making friends in that environment, as long as you get closer to the good ones and, in addition to your plans, you wish the good of the community you belong to.

It cannot be good to you if all around you are fallen to the ground. Help them through any correct methods and this good work will certainly return.

Find your friends through sports (gym, aerobics, jogging, swimming, yoga), hobbies (dances, photography), online (groups focusing on various interesting topics), social events.

Do charitable acts. We do not need someone just when we go through hard times, but we need each other because we are humans. We must learn and enjoy the experiences of life together. Help those in need.

Run away from people who do not respect their word. The world is full of all kinds of people. Surround yourself with professionals.

When I was a child, living in Săvârşin - Romania, trains fascinated me and often I was running to the train station, to see them. When the train station manager announced a train, through the loudspeakers that rang so far: *The fast train, one thousand seventy seven, from Timisoara, with the direction of Ilia, Simeria, Şibot, Alba-Iulia, Teiuş, Aiud, Războieni, Cluj-Napoca, Vatra Dornei, Campulung Moldovenesc, Vamă, Gura Humorului, Suceava, Paşcani, Iaşi ... arrives at the station, on line three. Attention to the line three!* Hearing these words, in my childish mind, poor in knowledge, I imagined that train as a kind of Trans-Siberian. Later, I learned that he was nicknamed "The Hunger". However, when he made his appearance, with the strong sound of the electric trumpets, engines, dozens of brakes and wheels, as big as it was, it seemed to break the earth. I imagined huge cities that will pass through, Şibot, Teiuş, Vatra Dornei. I was wondering how Vatra Dornei look like, what was there? Was a great question to me at the time. I imagined places by name. Even now, after I was in Teiuş, I cannot separate this name from the train whistle. Sighet seemed to me a very distant city. I associated his name with the snow, the North Pole, Santa Claus and the tiredness of the train drivers.

In the meantime, I have met people from almost all these places, some of them becoming very dear friends. The world is wide, do not limit yourself to where you live, make friends everywhere.

When I arrived at the high school in the city, in Timisoara, after living in Săvârşin, I felt like I had arrived in a metropolis. From the neighborhood of Circumvalaţiunii to Piaţa Rozelor, on foot, I had to walk an eternity. I am in London now, and Timisoara seems to me to be a small town. Life goes on, we change, adapt and learn.

Whatever you do you create, then you will have to live in the world you have created. Choose to spend time with people who inspire you, in places that inspire you.

Make a party and invite influential people to take part, invite reporters and journalists. There is no shame in having or acquainting yourself in many areas, as long as you do no harm somebody by using them.

Seek for help.

Look around for people or institutions that can help you on your way or they are created specifically for this. They exist, but they will not come to find you, this is your duty. If you do not tell me your thoughts, I cannot help you. You cannot wait in silence; you cannot wait for people to read your thoughts.

Once you recognize your values that will always keep you in the light, find models around you and begin to solidify your relationships, start and set your mind toward education. You cannot start on the road without knowing where you are heading.

CHAPTER 5

LEARN!

„An investment in knowledge pays the best interest." Benjamin Franklin

LEARNING GIVES YOU CONFIDENCE in your own strengths. The better you know what you do, the better you can make decisions and understand what is bad and what is good, but takes time. You have to give yourself time and energy to get what you want.

To become a doctor, you have to learn not only few years, how long the school lasts, but also many more years later. Where do you put the fact that, after a doctor learns and specializes, the medicine evolves, the medical equipment changes, the way the medicine is practiced changes, new drugs appear. Then, in order to become a teacher, you must learn, to become an electrician, welder, driver, you must learn. The more difficult is the activity you want to carry out successfully, the more you have to learn. Do you think business can run successfully without learning? Wrong! Those who do profitable business without learning are special cases or people at high risk. In order to become an investor, you must learn. You cannot go at risk, especially when you cannot afford to risk.

If you have not seen a horse in your life and you see a horse-shaped cloud in the sky, in fact, you see a simple cloud. If you are blind and touch a golden bulge, you will think it is a stone. Learn to understand what you see and what you hear, to distinguish gold from stones. Learn about sales, accounting, websites, marketing and so on. You need to know something about everything your employees will do.

Some people think it will be easier later, after all the other things will be arranged for them, but if you look clearly, it is always harder or even impossible later. The perfect moment does not exist. Learn now what you need to know for later.

Remember that the person who plants few seeds will have a small crop; the one who plants many seeds will have a large crop.

2 Cor 9:6

You cannot know yourself without self-education, as you do not know the earth without surrounding it or without learning much about it. If I had not seen the earth globe in different forms and no one would have told me that the Earth is round, I probably would not have undertaken astrology to discover the wonder. If I had started, I would have lost so much time for a lesson that I can now easily learn from some existing books.

Learn from books, learn from competent people, learn from free or paid courses, learn from religious books, learn from where you want. Knowledge will make you more tolerant, more modest and more intelligent.

Learn from your own experience. One of the ways is volunteering. If you have not done so by now, you probably do not have as much learning as you can. Ask questions, seek a mentor and make friends to learn from, find the right people, knowledgeable in

57

the field you are interested in. The reward is far more valuable than the money itself.

Learn with the Internet. Google is up and people still don't use it.

One day, in central London, I was waiting for someone, and a bus full of young people at the age of student stopped at the traffic light. A woman was talking on the microphone next to the driver. She was the guide of the group. I was amazed when the bus passed by me and I saw all the young people buttoning their cell phones, not even one was looking out the window. The bus had foreign plate numbers; tourists were probably for the first time in England, in central of London. Now, how many people use the Internet to its true value? Most are wasting their time on socializing pages, losing the real life, the real images and real events in the immediate vicinity. Use the internet, but do not become his slave! Then, taxes and online payments, communications... learn how to use 21st century tools, gaining time and energy. Learn about the online. Nowadays, online presence is mandatory.

As a small help, when you search for information online you may find different opinions. It only takes a little time to find the right source to give you an answer. Send an email and expect a correct and up-to-date response.

You need to take things seriously and learn about what you need. If you want to jump with a parachute, it is not enough to get a parachute. You have to learn about it, for your own safety. You have to read about it, learn from others and follow their movements, make a plan to know where you start, where you want to go, and how. Even if parachuting is a fun thing, you have to take it very seriously. It's the same in business.

The more you know, the better you calculate your risks, and they will diminish until they are almost gone, but anytime unexpected things can happen. When you have other people who depend on your business, you must always be prepared.

A smart man can learn from a fool.
Conversely's harder.

François Rabelais

Keep your mind open. If you do not know about some things, it does not mean they are not there. Be receptive to news and open to learning.

Learn about the legal side. Find out about laws, acts, institutions, rules, accounting. It is not enough to find people to help. If you know nothing about what they do, how can you choose a good one? By knowing the laws, you can avoid certain payments or you can get rid of all kinds of extra acts, within the limits of the law. If you do not know the law, you cannot exercise your rights.

You must also learn from those who have gone through experiences related to the field of your choice. In real life, some mathematical calculations do not fit, sometimes there are price reductions and sometimes you have to buy products that are more expensive because you are in a hurry. Sometimes 1 + 1 is not equal to 2.

Remember, the books cannot help you if you do not read them.

Develop your business skills, but be careful not to stay at this level. Set deadlines. Otherwise, you might still read for many years, but don't turn any idea into reality. Build yourself a space where you can learn and work, an office.

You do not have to be ashamed of your past failures, learn from them and move on.

I hailed you with so many exhortations to learn, but I am not talking about transforming someone into a street vendor, but about transforming yourself into a professional.

Be faithful in small things because it is in them
that your strength lies.

Mother Teresa

This day is over. We all learned either something, or we lazy. This is not your case; you have just completed an important chapter.

ANDY HERTZ

CHAPTER 6

MAKE WISE CHOICES

The world started with a trade,
because Adam sold Heaven on an apple.
It wasn't a great deal, really!

Honore de Balzac

I N ORDER TO RUN a profitable business, you have to master the meaning of these two words very well: income and expenses.

Income: money that is earned from doing work or received from investments (dictionary).

Is there any point in telling you what "expense" means? Yes! When you buy the most expensive tiles and a Jacuzzi bath for the bathroom of the house where you live, you make an expense. No way an investment, how could you have thought by now. Expenses are part of everyday life and everyone is familiar with them. Revenues, however, are a little harder to achieve. Revenues generally come from work or businesses that generate money. These are your assets. The more assets you have, the higher and safer your income is.

Assets may be real estate purchased for rent to other private or legal persons. Money from assets on a monthly basis is what passive income means. I mean, „No work". Assets can also be intellectual properties, businesses of any kind, even the personal education in which you invest is somehow still an asset. And it's the liabilities that consume your money. The car, the house you live in, the unused villa in the mountains and, in some cases, to make a joke, the life partner.

If you get to know the field you want to invest in better, you'll find out which part is investment and which speculation.

For example, in real estate, there is a claim when you buy an apartment with the idea of selling it more expensive over a while and buying it at market price in the hope that it will grow. But the investment is when you know that a major shopping Centre will open in the vicinity of that building or when you buy it at 75% of the market price. That is, 25% you already earn on purchase. Then you earn from renting, then you can sell it at a price of at least 100%. You have to differentiate between these terms, assets and liabilities, investments and speculating, so that you can do profitable business based on concrete data. It's not enough to be a businessman, you have to be a wise businessman.

When you increase your expenses (a child appears, you move into a larger house, you buy a better car and so on.), you don't focus on saving as much as you can produce more. You keep wondering where to cut, thus consuming your energy. Better put your mind to work and make the money you need. If you want a cabin in the mountains, buy one at a price at least 25% lower than the market level. Then look for a local businessman in that area. Offer him the key of the cabin and ask him for a monthly rent for your cabin so that investment pays itself back in 10 years. The businessman will find tourists for accommodation, but that doesn't interest you. You can use the cottage two months a year.

When you buy the house for yourself, it still has to be an asset. You increase its value or you buy it below the market price. Whether it's an apartment or a studio. Don't lose your mind about being a businessman in your spare time. When you go to buy the house where you will live, in addition to choosing the area, the design, the furniture, do not forget when you will have to sell it, in case this happens. Keep this in mind, both when you buy and when you want to make interior changes and all kinds of expenses.

Going back to business and choices, you have to begin from some point, but it's even more important to finish or to end that some point. It's a lot about starting a college, but it's more about finishing it. It's a good to start running for health, but it's even more important to do that every week, after 20 weeks of running.

Look for people already trained in the field you're starting to. For example, if you need a website, learn everything you can about it, but if you want someone to do it, call a professional. I learned that from personal experience. In the end, for a job well done, you will inevitably reach the professionals. If you don't search for them in the first place, you'll pay for the same service twice. If you want to do a good thing, do it right from the beginning.

Here's a simple example: in one of my apartments where tenants live, the boiler has broken down. As I had left the country for a long time, I asked the tenants to look for a plumber to fix it, then pay it, subtracting that amount of money from the rent they were going to pay me for the next month. Maintenance repairs like this I take on me as owner. Said and done. The work was done by a plumber friend of the tenant's family, after his work schedule, with the words „I did everything I could, as long as will work, will work". It cost 100 lei. In other words, it cost me 100 lei. Two weeks later the problem came up again. I told them to call someone else from a company. As the boiler was a „special one", they couldn't find a company in the city to solve the problem, but they found another „friend". It cost another 80 lei, the boiler was operational for a few more days only. It was a hot water problem, a sensor. Finally, I called the representative office of the boiler company that manufactured these components, based in Bucharest. They told me that they have workers in every county and they would send someone to fix the boiler sometime in the next day, after I explained the problem and its effect. The next day, the boiler was repaired by the professionals on that model, the defective part was not cleaned, but changed to a new one, they issued an invoice, they offered a guarantee on the work, and the price, how much do you think it was? 120 lei! So, don't think about saving money by calling on „after-hours friend". Call on professionals who take responsibility. Solve what needs to be solved faster, saving money, having guarantee and reducing your stress.

A wise choice is to be organized. Disorganization causes a lot of stress, for a number of reasons. One is that, not being organized, you forget. You forget to pay bills, you forget to call partners, you forget to send emails and you forget to go on a date. A business doesn't run like this. Another reason why disorganization causes stress is that, not knowing how much you have to do, not having a clear table of things to do, they seem to be much more than they are. Disorganization turns into disorder, which fatigues the mind and so on, follows a whole chain of problems amplified by a disorganized attitude. And on the other side, organizing greatly improves your life in general, clears your thinking and relieves you of a lot of stress.

Other wise choice is to use your talents. We all have inclinations towards skills or activities that become our passions and which we are better at than many others. Well, they have to be used. If all people would use them, we'd live in a better world. The idea is not to leave your passion as a weekend activity, but to try it into the activity that will bring you beautiful days and also money. Nowhere will you yield better than in that place that will make you wake up in the morning with love to get there with a smile on your face.

While many people argue about politicians – if they steal, how much they steal – or if they come sinister, where they come from, where they go, and so on ... they don't realize they can't find time to help others or help themselves. Waiting for the news on television, they no longer have time and clear minds for love, for people, for passions. During that time, others are acting. You don't have time this way for your loved ones and for your dreams. You get lost in a world that's not yours. What I don't understand is this: if some people care so much about what others do, if they spend hours in front of the TV to find out what's going on outside their environment, yet when they walk down the street and meet a hungry and sick man, why do they pass carelessly?

Television, gossip and laziness drive away the people from success. They focus on nothingness and lose the big picture of their life. They have busy minds, they are easy to manipulate and they are dependent and vulnerable.

Choose to make decisions and take responsibility for them, be mature in thinking, know your obligations and keep your promises. This way you can't fail if you're patient. Patience is not pleasant, but the results are very precious when you have patience.

The pension, it also goes into the chapter of wise choices. If you have enough income and you pay state pension taxes, that's fine. But that pension I don't know if it will cover your needs. Private pension? No! I would never put my money in a private pension, money that I didn't have full access to. Besides, I have no idea what's going to happen to that company in decades. I prefer to invest my money in real estate, which will bring money for retirement from rents. If you have too much money, invest in jewelry, artwork, land, real estate. You'll be able to redeem them in old age and there are deposits for your money, much safer than pension companies. It's my opinion.

Make wise choices and change the world for the better. I believe that together we can change the world, not through struggle, but through clean facts. Through small gestures, simple and sincere gestures, which, as a wave of goodness, will wash away the world of evil. Be a drop of this giant wave!

Here, on a few lines, is a conclusion about a few years of my life. So, in the few years of adulthood in which I felt the most protected, the most secure, the most comfortable, by looking back, I realize that I evolved the least, I lived the least, I felt the least and I built almost nothing.

And in the years when it was the hardest, in the years of uncertainty in my life, in the years of major change, I developed the most, I lived the most, I felt the most, I learned more than I thought I could, I built the most. Thus, "hard" does not mean "bad." Now, I'm looking to make full use of my time and resources so I can build more. Because it became fun. And I don't want to regret later that I wasted my years and my power. I'm doing the best I can. A life full of excuses does no good to me, to you, to others. We weren't born to feel sorry for ourselves, but we were born to win!

Make things happen so you love Monday as you love Sunday. Follow your dreams!

ANDY HERTZ

CHAPTER 7

GOALS AND VISION

IF YOU WANT TO live a monotonous life, put on light targets and you'll take small steps. If you want to live a life of ups and downs, with many accomplishments and chores and all sorts of experiences to tell your grandchildren, then aim away.

*For verily I say unto you, That whosoever shall
say unto this mountain, Be thou removed, and
be thou cast into the sea; and shall not doubt
in his heart, but shall believe that those things
which he saith shall come to pass; he shall have
whatsoever he saith.*

Mark 11: 23

Those who do not believe they can fulfill their dream, will never fulfill it. Logical. It's like I'm looking at a mountaintop, and then I'm telling myself I can't climb it. The result is that I won't even try, because I don't think I can get there anyway. If others pull me after them and every hundred meters they have to cheer me up, then the road is no longer pleasant, so it's not worth the effort. But when I think I can go up and tell myself that I will do this at any cost, the chances are the maximum to achieve, plus the road is pleasant. The pleasure of the road is the key to happiness, even in a relationship, in sport, in art, in business and others. If happiness lasted only during an Olympic athlete's awards ceremony, what would be said about the years of work, about passion, about dedication? Would it be worth the effort of so many years for a day of happiness? Not! But happiness lasts not a day, but all those years, then, endures through wonderful memories and other pleasant activities. That athlete, however, believed from day one in the dream of becoming a champion.

Fears to keep you away from your dream, away from your purpose, is life wasting!

Do you know how? It's like getting an hour of life and a mountain in front of you. Then, it's nothing. Therefore, if you go up or not, the time goes by anyway.

You either stay down or you go around in a circle, and you say that something might happen to you on the way up, or, you go up and you go, and you go, and you go, and you go, and you become unstoppable.

There's also a need for a plan. But a plan, no matter how good it is, if it's not put into practice, becomes useless. A plan, even not the best, but put into practice, becomes better than the very good one, forever postponed.

If I want to write a book and I tell myself I want to finish it in a year, I probably won't write it at all. If I want to write a book, I have to act, but before that, I set some simpler limits for a near future. Example: - Next week I have to write an hour a day. So, maybe I'll finish the book in half a year! The plan has to be general, and then, on each point, you have to set a clear schedule. Another example:

-This year I want to go to the gym more often. Ok. *Today no, tomorrow no*, and you end up not going. If you say *I have to go to the gym every Tuesday,*

Thursday and Saturday is different. Make clear plans with data. Write down your plans!

Yesterday (don't tell anyone), I peeked into the notebook of a woman who sat next to me on the train. I saw that after thinking a little, she wrote something, and then she thought again and wrote again. What was she doing? ...a list of things to attend to! I thought then about what simple list some people have. I have an Excel table divided into 12 pages, each for another domain. I'll tell you about it a little below.

Anyway, it's very good to make a notebook or a wish table. This will give you the opportunity to review your goals and to look for solutions to achieve them. Otherwise, you will forget about them, you will always be distracted to others to do and you will not act enough in achieving them. Think away, give your mind beautiful and big thoughts, then, write them down. You'll see later how much it matters.

Example of a table: I use an Excel table, about 5 minutes a day and it is very simple, which contains several pages, each dedicated to a domain. The first is called „Money" and is divided into many horizontal and vertical columns, colored differently depending on months and years. Entries from rents, expenses, debts, money lent to others, and so on. The second page is called „Banks", where I passed data related to the banks I work with, loans, deposits and their phone numbers. This data is entered only once, after that, it must be updated rarely. The third page is called „To Do", which is divided into „Various", „UK" and „Ro". In these tables I find everything I need to do, from calling someone, to the date impending my technical check on the car. Also on this page, I keep my goals, so I can see them almost every time I sit in front of the computer. The fourth page is dedicated to writing. It's called „Book" and contains everything to do about writing, publishing, contacts, ideas for a new book, title ideas and so on. I also have pages called „Company 1", „Company 2", „Silver", „2016" and so on. I know, it sounds complicated and hard, but I've gotten used to it since the time when this table had only one page. Now, I'm working on two monitors and I always open the Excel table on the right, even if then I cover it with other pages. I save it entirely, from time to time, on an external memory and that's all about it. It helps me very, very, very much in everything I do.

In Chapter 4 I talked a little bit about essential values, without which you can't set some clean goals.

These personal values not only help you find and to go on the right way, but also protect you. If you respect and love your family, one of the values you believe in may be to have dinner with your family every evening. By doing this, you keep the family together, you eat without haste, you learn about various problems of your loved ones, you reduce stress, plus, you're creating a new value for your kids.

Then, if your values are family, love, health, education, nature, then the opinions of others, praise and gossip will no longer matter.

Values help you in setting goals for the future. The cleaner and healthier your values are, the cleaner and healthier your goals will be.

If you don't do things for pleasure, how can they work in the future?

If you want to find reasons to complain to others about the hard life you have, you can do that in any country, in any city, in any village.

I know someone who always complains about the lack of money. Not today or yesterday, but as long as I can remember. But ever since then, this person lives the same as he did many years ago. Debts, money on the limit, more debts, more banks, more loans, for general expenses. Unpleasant work, nine hours a day, in a factory. A life that can be said to be hard, unhappy.

I wonder, if you don't change something, who's going to change your life for you? I also know some who earn very little, but they try to do all kinds of scams. Well, once you stop making them, the gain is lost, and if you don't stop, the gain is becomes small. Some continue to do what they don't want, they don't have enough money, they complain all the time, they wait for a major change from the outside, they live on the edge and they don't change anything about themselves. The saddest thing is that even they have no goals or a long-term vision either doesn't exist or it's a very sad story.

Believe me, if you don't set some clear goals and an action plan for your life, in 15 years, you'll be in a place either the same with this one from now on or in a worse one. Just with fantastic luck, things will work out for you from outside.

If you have the courage, wait for your luck. If you have wisdom and courage, make your luck!

Learn from mistakes. It's not that bad to make a mistake as it is to make a mistake second time. If you feel you're about to make second time the same mistake, ask others for help.

Never forget your motivation and goals. You can't go higher than you propose to yourself to climb.

Recently I was tempted to buy a cabin in the mountains. I felt like a child in front of the candy shop front window. In my mind, that creamy slice of cake was, in fact, a wonderful and very cheap cabin in a wonderful place. But I didn't deviate from my plan to have smaller, leased real estate. The thing is, after you set a goal, if you know it's good and you believe in it, try not to get out of the way. That mountain place is a wonderful dream for each of us, but it has to come as a result of money from profitable businesses, so that it doesn't tie me to a cart that consumes my energy, in some cases, for the rest of my life. The cabin's coming later.

Not believing in your dream is like not believing that you can give life to a child, or is like you kill him before he can exist. There are also people who want something very much, their dream is a nice and clean one, but they don't trust their own. What's more, they're afraid of external changes that can mess up their plans. I think you can already infer my opinion...

One of my goals is to become financially free. I started buying real estate with money raised from work. Then, with money raised from rents and work, then with money from rents, from the bank and from work. And, like that, I'm going forward. The beginning is harder, but when you get to three, four, five, six properties, which you rent, things start to get serious, but on the other hand, much more realistic and the final goal starts to get closer. That's one of my ideas for becoming independent. I wish to go to the mountains anytime, drink my coffee in the morning and read the paper what time I want, be able to write in the morning and day, when I'm full of energy. Of course, I don't want a free life where I can sleep and watch TV all day, but one where I can use my energy on what does make a good life.

How many properties do you need in order to stop working? Depends on how much you consume. If your baldness is $4,500 a month, then you need so much to produce that amount of the rents you collect. Depends on the location, the rent price, how much money you spend each month, so you stay at the same level of living as you did until you decide to stop working. In general, I recommend more than 8 studio flats. You think you can't have them? If you think so, find out that's what I was thinking in 2010, when I was living in rent and my only valuable asset was a 1995 car and a laptop. After I bought the first property, I told a friend I wanted to see if I could have 10. In the meantime, it has become a concrete goal to become financially free. It is a mindset!

After a long-dreamed vacation, you come home with no money and start over? After you buy a car, do expenses for it or rates become a burden? If you want to take a course, do you have to borrow money to pay for it? If you answered "Yes!" to these three questions, you certainly already realize that you are on a path that needs to be changed. Start to the future with clear images of your destination. Start every day, in the morning, looking at the picture of your dreams. What kind of day is that started with news about problems, poverty, famine? You need to know what's going on in the world, but start the day with energy, be positive! Schedule your mind with something you want, so you can get better in your work, whatever you do that day. You will always have the destination in your mind and, for this reason, you will look for solutions that, sooner or later, will start to appear.

For your body, it's not what you don't eat, it's what you eat. And it's not what you don't drink, it's what you drink.

For your life, it's not so much what you don't want, it's about what you want. And it's not so much what you don't do, it matters what you do.

Every day...

If you see the future in a dark light, you create this reality that you almost feel. If you imagine your destination every day as a dream, you almost feel it. The more you feel it, the more energy you will receive and give so that you can get where you want to arrive.

You come home from work, in the evening, tired, no mood to play. Kids jump into your arms and ask you to play with them. What's to be done? I have an acquaintance who has two children, a wonderful wife, but little free time. And he bought two houses in London with money borrowed from the bank. Quite large amounts, which he will most likely not pay until retirement, if he worked until then in the same way, i.e. even 6 or 7 days a week. His salary's going to stay

BECOME A KING OR REMAIN A PAWN

pretty much the same, so he's on the edge of money every month. I don't think the week will reach eight days, so he can't earn more. His life will be dedicated to working to get money for the bank. What will he do when the powers will leave him? There are always several ways to solve a problem, and this is a big one. The ultimate sacrifice, life! Life given to work, 7 days a week, unpleasant, tiring work, for some objects. The solution is change, not randomly, but a well thought out plan. You need a goal, a clear goal. £600,000? How can you make this money? First daily, tiring, unpleasant work, working for another man's dream for the next 30 years, or through a business? Or you better work for 5-6 years, learn and do your best, and then do what you love. Either way, you'll have what you've created. A well-known man who works extremely hard, after a discussion about money, said to me "I'm so tired at night, I don't feel like learning, reading". Well, what does that mean, you're never going to learn anything again, and the road you're going to be the only one you know already?!

Learn and become free, addiction and laziness can destroy happiness and fulfillment!

The beaten road leads to where others have arrived, your road leads to where you want to go!

Take things where you want, don't stop in the middle of the road. You know, if you want to cross a busy road, when you get halfway you don't stop to run back, do you? Firstly because your goal is to pass, second, for the risk of being run over by a car; in the third, because time would be wasted. Stop yourself only when you feel that you're on the wrong path, but don't go back, just change direction.

> *I want to sing like the birds sing, not worrying about who hears or what they think.*
>
> *Rumi*

Passion, passion, passion! If you don't get to give your life to your passions in a way or another, you've lived for nothing! Aim to do what you want, create what you want, as long as you don't hurt others to achieve your goals. Some will say you're crazy if you follow your call. There are many people, right around us, who are convinced that you have to do what everyone else does, otherwise there's something wrong with you. If these opinions matter to you, you can be sure that your goals, values and vision are polluted. Don't listen to those who don't do a lot, it's not good to care very much about the opinion of those who don't resonate with you. You have to do what you feel.

Think far away ahead, give your mind beautiful and big thoughts, then write them down. You'll see later how much it matters.

Always view your destination and trust yourself!

An interesting goal may be for you doubling your free time. Another is to have as much free time as you want. Another can be career-related or passion-charity or family, and so on.

Once you identify your goals, do a little bit each day to achieve them. Don't think they're far into the future and you'll get started later. Start doing something today, however small.

Imagine that you could get to that point where you regret that you're not the man you could have become. Start with the first step and invent your life! The universe grows what you plant. Plant clean and beautiful thoughts!

ANDY HERTZ

CHAPTER 8

WORK

*Nothing great was ever
achieved without enthusiasm.*

Ralph Waldo Emerson

WERE YOU BORN TO do what you're doing today?

I. worked a lifetime on trains. G. has cut wood for as long as he knows. V. has been working in an office for years, and barely has time to make a phone call a day for personal gain. Most people get a salary, just enough to earn a living, and if they still tie their heads together with loans for some personal needs, they tie a cannonball to their feet, probably for life. Unfortunately or fortunately, not many people are doing very badly. Why "unfortunately"? When you're warm, you're afraid to make a change, so you don't give the warm seat to someone you don't know anything about. When you're doing badly, you're forced to make a change, which can only be for the better. When you're not doing very well, but you're not doing badly, you don't really know what to do and you wait, wait, wait...

I have a friend who doesn't love his job, but doesn't feel threatened there and earns pretty well. For years, he's been telling me how many plans he has, how much he wants to do, how he'd quit his job, but he doesn't have the guts. Beyond the words, practically, meanwhile, he took a pretty big loan from a bank for an apartment and car. Now he's in an even worse situation. He's not doing it badly, but he's not doing well, his needs for a modest life are covered, but even if he wants to leave his job and do more, he couldn't, because those bank rates have to be paid month by month. Otherwise, he dreams of early retirement. That's it. End of story.

If you want to do something more than you've done so far financially, you have to do something else than you've done so far. If you continue to do what you have done so far, without an unsuspected gain or a legacy that has fallen from the sky, things will not change considerably in years to come, and you will find yourself in the same place.

You sell your life, your hours, for money and to fulfill another man's dream, braver than you.

The job that doesn't fill your soul with joy, rather depresses you, makes you sick. The place where you're not your boss.

Someone said to me, "I don't know what I want, but I know what I don't want." That's a good quote! Even if you don't know what you want, it's good to know what you don't want. It's good to know whether or not you want to work a lifetime to buy things you don't need. It's good to know that maybe you don't want to get into old age without having lived your dreams in the meantime.

The reason you keep going the wrong way could be the fear of change?

You've probably realized from past chapters of this book my opinion that a job doesn't make sense if you don't love with all your heart what you're doing there. The reasons are many. One of them is that, having a job, you have to execute someone else's orders. You have to ask him or her to let you free for half an hour to solve a personal problem or sometimes you have to do things you don't believe in with all your heart or enjoy.

Time spent at work is a time sold out when work is not your passion. Hours and days, months and years, you have to spend so precious time there, in the place where you are not fulfilled and happy. I have friends who, after years, have stayed in the same work place. Same problems, same stories, same habits. Years pass, life passes. It is very sad that your happiness and dreams depend on some of other people's decisions.

You have certainly seen people who work very hard and yet remain poor and sad. Have you ever seen a monkey in a cage? It jumps all over the place, climbs the branches, goes on the ropes, incessantly. After hours, days, months, years of efforts in climbing, it is found in the same cage. The only significant change is aging. The action is useless when it is not used in the right place. Until you find the way to start with enthusiasm, your energy will be lost for purposes whose results will always be lower than you can give to the world. You'll thank your boss, you'll get a raise, you'll get a pat on the head, you'll get little gifts, you'll get promotions, but you'll never do anything extraordinary by your existence. I'm speaking in general. Of course there are jobs you can want and can't do on your own. If a man is passionate about research in a particular field, he can't do that at home or on his own. But if work doesn't make you happy, you can't be yourself in that position. Instead of waking up in the morning with a smile on your face, you wake up tired, lacking energy and enthusiasm, knowing you have to go to work.

Rushing to work, rushing in breaks, rushing home doesn't let you feel alive. You give up the sweet sleep of the morning, to run to the place where you do not feel alive. Your smile is not the natural one.

Not once did I call an acquaintance who said, „I can't talk, I'm at work, I'll call you later." He later calls: „I'm on the rush, I have to get home, but I still have to run there and there." Sad! Is that life?

The good news is this: you can make more money with your business than that „safe money" you get in the workplace. But you, no and no. You prefer to work to fulfill someone else's dream by giving up your dream. Let me tell you a little bit about T. who worked for others and is happy when he steals something or could sleep at work. Now, decades later, it does the same thing. He's stealing his hat. Take another nap, have another beer and, slowly, he's almost gone. A full life and hard work and thefts, time and screws. He lives in a state house, in a village, and he lives from today to tomorrow! T. built dreams for others.

Another, M., made tens of thousands of euros abroad, then built a large, double-decker house that never ends. There's always some work to be done, and he has to work incessantly, from morning to night, for his house, which is way too big. A few rooms are sitting empty. He used quality materials and put his soul into every corner of the house, which is why, he says, „doesn't deserve to sell it now". What he doesn't say is that he will never recover the money „invested" or the work done there. Thus, he remains trapped in this daily circle of work for a building that consumes incessantly, for nothing. Is it worth going to work for a lifetime for this reason?

If you find yourself in a position where you can't start a business yet, but you want to prepare your ground, even though you still have a job, don't think about the general way and don't wait a moment to start, but start now. Use your free time. That'll make the difference, and the moment you get to the point of leaving work for your business, you'll be on a roll. For example, I taught myself to build a website and it took me two weeks, an hour or two, a day. I didn't do this for lack of money, but out of curiosity. I wondered how to do it, what's so hard about it? Then I realized everything I wanted. It's not hard, it takes a while, but it's worth it. Because in the future, when you will have an online store, you'll know what it's about, when a problem occurs or your employees will tell you that "it can't be done".

...or you can lose the job you don't love anyway. Don't despair! It's the best thing that can happen to you. A change that, under other circumstances, maybe would not have come. How to find a new job? It's not the subject of this book, but I can tell you one thing: look for your passion, then look for a job related to it. Don't look for any job first, don't look for a better salary. Look for fun and a place to feel good, to give the world your energy and positive actions, a place to clear your mind and gather your strength.

People are blinded in bad jobs, with a raise of a few percent or small gifts. Do you know what it's like to work eight or nine hours in a toxic environment? When I say „toxic environment" here, I don't mean poisons or chemical products, but the place that, in one way or another, you destroy your physical and mental health. Either because your manager is aggressive, or because of stress, or because you feel like you don't belong there, or because there are no rules, and so on.

When I was in charge in a factory, where even pregnant women worked hard, I had no idea there were other solutions. It was only, in time, that I found my way out of that job, through a new business with silver jewelry. Fear of change kept me on the wrong track until I realized it was worse not to make any changes. Then I discovered that I could be free and earn more money, and that life was not designed for a man to spend time in a place where he doesn't feel happy. That is a struggle for survival, not life and joy at all. When you give your time and energy of life for money to buy food and a roof over your head, you live pretty much for nothing.

I was talking to a lady at an institution in London. The discussion went to work, and she said to me with a sigh:

-Oh... we have to have a job!

-Why is that? I asked.

-Because everyone has a job, how else? She replied in wonder.

-Everyone who chooses to have a job, has a job. But you, if you sell your house in London, you can live a lifetime, belly in the sun, in another country, probably in Indonesia. Bali sounds very good... This is an example, I said, maybe it's not the best, but here you are forced to have a job, it is your choice.

After a few seconds of silence, she changed the topic.

However, if you choose to have a job and you think it's better for you than to start working on your own, then at least choose a job that will bring you happiness and fulfillment. If you want to work in research, arts or any other field that involves passion, then do everything you can to get there.

Instead, if you say you want any job, it means you don't know what you want or don't know about any field of activity very well. If you don't know what you want, you have to go back to your passions. If you're not good at anything, then you have to learn.

So, if you go to an interview, you need to know one thing: for companies it is not easy to find the right people! They say no one is irreplaceable, but believe me, the management of any company has a lot of trouble finding the right people or almost suitable for the jobs. Any company owner wants the right employees. This means that the employees have to learn easily, adapt, be sociable, responsible, active, and so on. Become the right employee and you'll see how easy you'll find a job. Don't look at the job as a source of income. Look for a job you like, that will make you jump out of bed in the morning.

Well, when you get to the interview, for the job you choose wisely, assure them, whoever's holding the interview, that you're the right person. Don't wait them to ask questions, explain how much you want to work there and why. Make them sure you will work to raise the company and give examples of ideas that you've previously thought about when you've studied about the company that called you for an interview. Most of those who do an interview are taking it too emotional. If you know that job suits you, you have nothing to worry about. They want you more than you want them!

Propose that they agree you to work for them for a month on the minimum wage, so you can show them what you can do. Do you have the courage? I'm sure they'll hire you!

Insists that you love your chosen domain and you want to do something great there, because that's what you like to do. You're not just looking for a job to come home from, you're looking for a job to get away from home!

To come back to our topic, it's like this: variants exist, we have to find them. It's a game that not many people play. Most people choose the simplest way, but also the hardest, they accept what they gets in their life on the way to the end. The „tricky way" is hard for a while. If you don't work for yourself now and take some risks, you'll work for others for the rest of your life.

A few years ago, I was working in a factory and I had about 150 people under my control, I said. I had some wonderful colleagues, but we all, because of the stress and the high workload, in our spare time, at gym, at coffee, on weekends or on vacation, we were just talking about work. It became an obsession, a stress, a way of life. We also worked in night shifts, sometimes during the day we would stay in courses paid for by the company, believing that they would develop our way of thinking. In reality, we were mentally programmed to work harder and better for them. They were „educate" us. On the one hand it was true, we developed skills. Not for our own benefit, but for the benefit of the company. They were turning us into robots. One day, I realized I had to go. I didn't know exactly what I wanted to do, but I knew that's where I don't want to stay anymore. After I quit my job, which, after long discussions, was hardly accepted, I even started to receive arguments from my family like „So, one of this royal job you will don't get again" or „You don't even know what you're giving up, well you were there". I don't want to go into details. I went to do something else on my own. I mean, from work to someone else, to work for me. It was a fantastic experience. That's how I got to see what freedom looks like. I got to love Monday mornings. I started having breakfast in peace every morning. Then I had time to enjoy my coffee. I didn't have to go to bed early in the evening, because in the morning I could wake up at will.

Well, you know what some people are going to say? If we all left our jobs, who would work in factories or companies? Answer: will work the many, who do not read such books, who do not learn and do not want to believe that there are options. Regrettably, they will work for others, the others happily ever after!

If your job isn't pleasant and you don't feel happy there, here are a few lines that can make you think about or there may be signs of the need of change:

- You don't like what you're doing there.
- It's a toxic environment.
- Your work schedule is uncomfortable.
- You feel the need for a career change.
- You earn less than you need.
- You don't feel good at work.
- You don't have fun at work.
- The work environment does not correspond to your values.
- The work environment pulls you down.
- It gives you a lot of stress.
- You do not get along with your superiors or colleagues.
- You don't develop yourself intellectually.
- You get bored during the program.
- You feel that you have no personal life.
- You can't advance.
- The safety conditions are poor.
- There is no price on your opinions.
- You don't feel respected.
- You're criticized often.
- You are never told „Thank you!"
- You feel like you don't have a point.
- You feel that you don't matter to your boss.

- You can't develop your creativity.
- It has nothing to do with any passion.
- You do not go to work with enthusiasm.
- There's nothing left to learn.
- You hate your job.
- You love Friday more than Monday.
- Your health is affected.
- It negatively affects your privacy.
- You get more tasks than you can do during the program.
- Your colleagues are starting to leave the company.
- Your body tells you that you don't belong there.
- You have lost interest.
- You're wasting too much time on your way to work.
- There's too much gossip around.
- Real communication doesn't exist.
- You've been waiting for a promotion for years.
Or just...
- You want to work for yourself!

So if you want to quit your job and take responsibility for building a business plan on your own, you need an escape plan first.

If you realize that your job is not one that brings you joy, not helps you evolve, or it not makes you give the best of the world, then you have to give it up. You have to run away from the place where the time of your life passes pointlessly. But change must come at the right time, not overnight. Things like this need to be thought of and planned in advance. Before you go on your new path, you can take out a bank loan to start a business you already know enough about to what you're getting yourself into, or you can first raise a sum of money to make a living for the next few months or years. You can't throw yourself into the unknown, because it's not enough to dream, you have to live. For that, you need money.

CHAPTER 9

THERE WILL BE MUCH TO DO

IT'LL BE HARD WORK!

As a business grows, it also goes through stages of fall. You have to be prepared and you have to be aware of the hard times that might follow. A business is not a line that goes up indefinitely, but has ups and downs.

You can expect along the way you are going, financial crises, legislative changes, problems of any kind. As I said in a previous chapter, 1+1 is not equal to 2 at all times. You may also be going through moments of depression. If that happens, you need to know that depression is the sign that your body tells you need a break. With this sign you realize you need to reset something, then you start doing what you think is best for you. Depression is like the sting in your belly that you feel when you run too much and is meant to stop you from running. If there wasn't that sign, you can run until you die. Appreciate these signs and listen to them. Your body will always show you if you're going the good way or the wrong one.

You can still expect problems with people, whether employees or collaborators. I'm telling you honestly, so I don't have to say any more possible problems: so many evils can happen, that I could fill an entire chapter with them. But what does it matter? One problem may occur along the way, another may occur, or perhaps another one, and maybe a monster is hiding right under your bed! Go ahead!

All you need to know is that problems can occur, so they need to catch you as ready as possible and you have to solve them as much as you can. That's it.

About periods of recession: there are cycles of decline and rising economic activity. We have seen businesses that were born in times of economic crisis and businesses that died in high economic times. It depends a lot on how you run a business. For example, it is true that, in times of crisis, the mountain hostels will no longer be occupied in too large a percentage, but if you offer something new at your hostel, there will be many people who will come to you even in times of crisis. Renting saves real estate in times of financial crisis. You can't control the country's economy, but you can control the revenue generated by a property of your own.

If you are irritated by every rub,
how will your mirror be polished?

Rumi

At the moment I live in rent, although I have several properties rented. If you have a large family and you want to buy a house of your own, of course you have to do that and it deserves all the comfort you choose. But as long as you choose to stay in rent, that's also fine.

Some say you can't find tenants everywhere except in big, rich cities. I, from the moment I bought the first property to be leased, there was no time to lack tenants during the financial crisis. Here it depends a lot on how you know to find what you need. On the news I have seen jobs crisis, the closure of factories, the decrease in the number of students, the landlords in search of tenants, and I, ...I was getting e-mails like, „Don't you know something to rent in the long run?".

103

Imagine that, before the crisis, you bought a studio to be rented (an asset) with 100 units. After a year its price dropped to 80 units. If you rented it for 1 unit a month, in five years you made 60 units. By lowering expenses, you're down to 40 units. The financial crisis is over, you have a good worth ex. 90 units, growing, plus 40 units in your pocket. Total 130 units. Growing, of course!

Tenants must be kept for long. First of all, they're not numbers, they're people. You have to make sure they're okay. If they're well, you're well. What would you do to keep at every six months an empty property for a month and, until the next lease, lose a month of profit? If that happens twice a year at ten properties, you lose 20 months of profit. What do you have to do to keep your tenants? Pay attention to them and be friends with them. Help them and give them the chance to help you too. Think about the fact that you're lucky enough for people to get into your life. Enjoy this fact and appreciate it!

Give them presents! Buy furniture or upgrade some of the property. You're the one with the money, they're the ones who need a living space. The rent for the two months I was talking about above reinvests one in the rented property. Or at least the rent for a month. They will greatly appreciate this.

Then, when you feel lost, when you go through a difficult moment, your energy disappears. You're losing your confidence and your powers. If during that time you found out, for example, that you had won the Lotto or that a loved one was coming from far away to see you, you would jump up for joy, you would have all the strength anymore. What does that mean? It means that your power already exists within you, and your mind, depending on external factors, intensifies or shackles it. Attitude to external factors makes the difference. These factors can either destroy your life or fill it with energy. Your attitude makes a difference, but it requires long discipline. Nothing comes overnight.

I have already talked about fears, but I can also say that many are more afraid of life than of death. You don't have to give in to thoughts that drag you down and make you tremble in the face of problems. Try to see life as a game. Its rules include solving challenges.

There are people who lose their family for nothing, because of fears.

You must also know that we are not equal. Some have to work harder than others to reach a level of equality. I gave myself years of my life to get to where others already were. But I'm making this comparison for you, so you can learn from this. I'm much higher

than I was a few years ago and that's enough for me –
it's the only comparison I make for myself.

Before you start a business, it's good to be aware
that it can happen that doesn't have a long life. Either
the market is tired or you can't adapt to the
requirements. In good time, save money. Of course,
you will start another business if the first one does
not meet your expectations, but if you produce
considerable amounts, put money into assets for
later.

Don't throw money at cars, watches and houses
from immediate profit. Reinvest in yourself and in
your company. The expenses for „whims" will be
made from the money from the assets acquired from
the business. Example: you opened a car wash
company. After you buy a studio flat from your profit
and it produces rent, that rent gathered in a few years
can bring you holidays, a new car, and so on.
Anyway, I hope you're not looking for perfection, but
fun.

Whatever happens, don't give up!

Getting into business also means taking
responsibility. I want to tell you something for your
real relationship with future employees, because you
might create jobs. You run away from a job, but you
give that thing to others? Make a difference, just

because you stopped by. Remember what you didn't like about your old job when you hire someone in your business. Understand people, but chooses the best. Don't choose people who work cheaply, choose people who are good at what they have to do, people who make with passion those things useful to your company. Hire properly, so they deserve what you'll be happy to offer. And even if they leave, just like you left, it's better to have a good team than a mediocre, lazy team forever.

In some areas you can work with sellers on a commission basis, but make sure they are good at what they do. And focus on the idea of giving back to the world, of giving back help that you maybe got, even if it wasn't a material one. Create jobs for those who want to learn and become better and for those who need a start, not money.

I was helped too, I was offered confidence and support. Maybe not as much as I would have liked or maybe not in the way I was waiting, but I got help. All things are done together, even if you can't see it. Help others. Don't just count your losses, consider you turning a favor to the world.

Help any people who gets in your way. Help them learn. Don't give food to the one who can earn his own food, unless you give him a dream, a purpose, a tool that he can manage later without you. Pick up people, don't fuel their poverty.

107

Inspire people! Get them up! Make their lives better! After all, if you don't change other people's lives for the better, you can say you didn't make much on Earth. What are you doing for the others at the moment?

Don't forget that between your dreams to imagine the moment when you do something good for humanity.

Then, you'll be successful! If that's what you're after and you're going to have, that's what you're going to have! How many times have you heard someone say that? Most people are not successful, because they are afraid of success.

CHAPTER 10

GET MONEY

BEING A BUSINESSMAN IS not about having money, it's about knowing how to use money.

First of all, this has to go right into your head: „Don't make money at all cost!" Throughout your journey through life you must remain honest and with a good reputation!

That being said, if you want to work for yourself you have to get some money, in addition to many other things to do. If you think that's easy, you're right, if you think it's hard, you're right. If you think it's hard, I'm telling you that it's harder to work a lifetime on other people's dreams and between fixed hours.

Let's talk a little bit about money and what can happen. I'm going to start with a real and sad story. The moment Ms. E. asked me to borrow them a large sum of money, especially for a couple of pensioners who were having a hard time, I had no idea that, in a short time, they would be homeless because of their debts.

She called me one day, in 2009, to tell me that they urgently needed 700 euros, but without her husband knowing this, because he had a heart condition. Knowing them as good people, I brought the money, meeting her without her husband's knowledge, on a street corner, like criminals. After a brief discussion from which I understood nothing, she promised to return the money after a week, asking me again to keep secret from Mr. G., her sick husband. I was surprised by the situation, knowing that, not so long ago, they borrowed a considerable amount from the bank to renovate their apartment, although I did not see very large changes in their apartment.

I would sometimes visit them, having a shared passion with Mr. G., in the field of electronics. He was good at it, being a former communications director in the years of communism, a sign that they had led a good life in the past.

Well, it's been over a week and Ms. E. hasn't called. When I called her, to ask about the money, she started crying, saying that she had to get a sum of money from somewhere else and asked me to have a little patience. Finally, I recovered my money in five tranches, hardly stretched over a period of a few weeks.

Not long after, Ms. E. called me and invited me for a coffee at their house to talk about something, all three of us. Very surprised, I got there after a few hours. They were both crying. Seeing an old man crying when he's not even close to you, as a family is, is a rare experience. He blamed her, speaking jerkily, as he wiped away his tears. She didn't wanted to talk. I sat in an armchair, under a library, between two cabinets, next to a table covered by a sewn tablecloth, on which it was waiting for me a coffee in a small cup, next to a plate replacing an ashtray. Mr. G. sat on the couch, and Ms. E., on a small three-legged seat by the window. In the silence broken by only a few sobs, I lit a cigarette whose smoke covered the entire room in a few seconds, a rather small living room from an apartment in the style of a wagon.

-I'm listening to you! I said, in the tone of a teacher who is going to examine the students.

-Tell him what you got us into! Mr. G snapped.

Ms. E. pulled out a cigarette from an old style pack of cigarettes, lit it up and started the story.

One day, she had no money in the house and thought of borrowing 100 euros from a neighbor, with the thought that she would return the money when the pension arrives. Since their money wasn't enough in generally, she took 300 euros from somewhere else to pay back 100 euro back and have something left. Then she took 1000 euros from one of the children, to give back the 300 euros and stay with the rest of the money. Then she took 1500 euros from someone else to give back to the her son the 1000, then she took 2000 euros from somewhere else and so on, without Mr. G.'s knowledge, until she took 4000 euros from a loan shark. I'd already lost the string and the thread of things... That's when the problems began, and the reason why Mr. G. also found out about their situation as a family. Together they took 4000 euros from another loan shark, through loan documents on which the sum was 5000 euros. 1000 euro more, the part of the second loan shark. This 4000 euros were returned to the first loan shark. After a few months, the contract deadline expired, and they didn't have the money to pay back, 5000 euro. The children could not help them, and the second loan shark was following some legal procedures in order to sell their apartment. Because of the shame and because they don't wanted to move on the children's heads, they asked to stay in rent, in their „former" home, lost for a sum of nothing, compared to its price, about 12000 euro. They called me to tell someone about the trouble and ask for advice. It was too late. It's very sad to see two elderly people, desperate, asking for help. On the other hand, this was a very good lesson for me, which is not to take loans when, with the help of money, I do not make a profit greater than interest.

Between people, one is physical attraction and one is love. With money it's the same, you're attracted to money or you do things with passion. There's a difference in having money just to have money and having money for a passion you want to develop.

Money's not a problem! The way you use money can become a problem. You can get a fabulous inheritance or win the Lottery and, in a few years, lose everything. Or you can have few dimes to turn into millions. It depends on how you think, how you use money, how you put your money to work.

How long takes to get 10,000 euros?

I'll answer you: it depends on who you ask. For some it takes the price of a phone, for others, decades of work. It's very important the circle of people you're in, your contacts, your reputation and so on. To have access in circles of influential people, you have to have some qualities. You can't wait for this to happen at home, you have to work and go out. There are people who get money in the blink of an eye, because others know them as trustful people. There are others who, in times of trouble, have nowhere to get little money, because no one gives them. This aspect raises questions about those people. If I know I can get the money today from a bunch of places, how can another man not be able to get money out of nowhere, not even for a pair of pants?!

To start a business, you need money. Not necessarily too many. Not necessarily yours. However, it is best to have your money and, of course, how many as possible. You also have to think about the time between opening a business and when it starts to make a profit. For example, a businessman when opening a hotel, calculates the cost of the investment plus losses for a period of time, in which he does not make a profit. Where do you get the money to start the business? From parents, friends, investors, shareholders. How do you get the money? Today is easier than in the past, your luck!

The first source, the most reliable and sincere, in some cases, are the parents. When they can help you, they're the first ones to turn to. I don't think it's right to put pride on the first place. On the bright side, they're not going to punish you, they're not going to press you.

Another source of money is the house you live in. If you have a good deal in mind, why not sell your house? In some cases, it's a good option. For example, you want to open an online store. There is no need for online stores to be created in large cities. If you live in a big city, where the maintenance of a house or apartment costs a lot, you can move to a smaller city, and with the money you get from the sale you will buy a bigger one and start the business you want, without debt.

Another source of income is working abroad. In general, because I know the case, many eastern Europeans work in Western Europe. Most of them consume a lot of money from the gain, especially the young ones. Almost all the money goes on monthly expenses, rent, entertainment, clothing and cars. Some, however, raise money. They learn the language of the country where they work, study, look for well-paid jobs, „pull hard" for a few years, then return to their country and start businesses. So a source of money to start a business can also be the fat porcelain piglet. Don't focus too much on saving money, though, but on getting money. No rich man has been employed for too long.

If you need money for a well-thought-out business, it's no shame to borrow money. But don't make the mistake of taking any interest, just to see

115

yourself with the money in the bag. On the day of payment, monthly, will be hard for you and every penny will matter. If you don't borrow for pointless expenses, it's a good thing to borrow money. For example, I, at the moment, am in debt to three banks in London, and all the money taken from the bank and invested in real estate that generates a monthly profit.

Attract partners

That's why you need to think your business more broadly. The business in your mind will not be only yours, but the fun will be appropriate if you find quality people to join you. There are many who have money and are looking for people with good ideas and energy to put them on the roll. Where do you find them? At events, conferences or various gatherings organized precisely so people get to know each other and find their possible business partners. You have the opportunity to expose your plan to them, in which you believe and for which you are willing to work very hard. You might earn them as partners, investors, collaborators. In finding partners you need to give respect and trust. Trustworthy people like to do business with other trustworthy people.

Partners can be found also among family or friends. Many will tell you not to interfere with others. I'm telling you that most of the people who made a lot of money, made them in a team, and then or at the end broke up.

Another idea is to get the money with the help of money. For example, you're hunting real estate. Borrow an amount, buy a bargain, sell, refund the amount, and start your business with the rest. Or you can access government funds designed to help people start a business. Some ideas involve you going into research. In the case of sales of services businesses, the starting costs are very low, so you can get money in several ways. If you want to start an interior design, consulting or cleaning company, you need very little. We'll talk about business ideas in the next chapter.

As I said above, there are many people from Eastern Europe who have gone to work in Western Europe. If you are one of them or you have this for your future, I wish you stability and happiness abroad. But if you can't adapt, you'll have to make a good plan to get back home. Think on long-term, don't delude yourself that, for now, you're making enough money, wherever you are. I think anyone in the UK, for example, in six months, a year or two years, can raise £10,000. Easier, harder, it can. With this cash, you can start a business for example in Romania. The poorer your place of return, the lower your start-up costs will be and the easier you will began. I mean villages, towns or small cities. Depends on the deal you want to do. Just think about the rent price for a space dedicated to your business, then the rest of your expenses, and you'll be able to choose the right place to do your business.

And, of course, you can raise even more money abroad!

When we have money, we have to use it in a healthy way. Even if you end up with a large amount of money obtained from work, by loan or as a gift from your loved ones, spend and invest with wise judgment. When you have to pay a small amount for something, imagine that only those are the only money you have. Don't throw your money out the window, especially because you might end up on the day you need to borrow, maybe, again.

Here's an example of a business that's gone, a negative example. A very capable guy, along with his brother-in-law and a friend, with help from his parents, built a beautiful and large cabin in a mountain resort in Romania. A wonderful area, surrounded by fir forests, ski slopes for the winter season, superb for hiking in summer. In the years before the financial crisis, around 2005, the business was doing excellent. The place was always full of tourists, food, coffee, drinks and flowed non-stop to the diners. Occasional tourists, school camps and revelers for the holiday seasons or weekends ...everything seemed to go better than in any original plan. What did our man think? Well, he thought, living the joy of a promising business for a few years, that, after the bank loans already made, he would borrow another sum of money to compensate the other two associates, so that he would be left alone in the business. Said and done. After paying a large sum to the parts of his partners, our man saw himself master of the money factory. But in 2008, after other loans, an expensive car, all kinds of investments in the building, mortgaged apartments, debts, came the crisis about which we all learned one way or another. I could lengthen the story, especially to the wonderful nature side around and the superb time that I spent there, but what we're interested in now is that our subject has run out of nothing and owes it to life. From a super-profitable business, he ended up in a situation from which not many manage to come out. Here is a man I consider capable, intelligent, educated and has gone broke because of an economic crisis that he has not considered. Because of this, I repeat, take care of every penny. Don't get carried away, eternal profits don't exist. There is always change, there is a need for adaptation and continuous education.

There is a saying: „Where does a thousand go, the hundred goes". It's a stupidity! Take care of the money!

I have another interesting story about money. I know a very rich man in London. Although he owns many real estate properties in the UK capital. He and his family have been looking into rent in a five-bedroom house for several years. Why is that? Because his properties are rented with the double rent he paid for the five-bedroom house. And another reason, because he couldn't find a house worth buying for his own comfort until recently. Now, he lives in an enormously expensive house, but it gives him the possibility of modifications to increase the space and number of rooms, so that if he were to think of selling it, after some modifications work, he could quietly ask for much more than he gave on it. We're talking about millions of pounds. A businessman remains a businessman, all the way. When this kind of people negotiate a million-pound house, and when they negotiate the price of a bike, and when they raise the seemingly insignificant penny found on the street they do the same, appreciating every penny. But especially when buying a property for its own use, property that normally does not bring profit, it can even become a big consumer. An intelligent businessman waits patiently until the right moment comes, like a crocodile waiting for his prey. He doesn't throw himself around anything that comes his way. Thus, it can turn a passive good into an asset. A good „money eater", it turns it into a good profit maker. In a few years, he will be able to move into an even bigger house and he will be left with money to spend for the rest of his life.

It matters a lot what you let come to you, even thoughts I mean, it matters a lot what you put to your heart. It can be said that in the world there is no „bad" and „good". In fact, there is only the perception of bad or good. Maybe I believe in the fact that having a tree in front of the house brings bad luck and it's bad and you think it brings good luck and it's good. That's pretty much how it is in everything. If you get to see things from a certain perspective, there's no pain. If you choose to rent your house and move in rent, that's your problem. Maybe you'll be left with some money and, based on the rent you get, you can borrow money from the bank for another house. Everyone knows his own. Then you can sell the car you work for maybe an hour a day and reduce your working hours by one hour. You'll have more time to make your plans for the future and you'll also have money to start with. The world has started to work more and more for „more", although not everyone really needs what they buy.

When you reach the level you want, you will take your car back. Attention! You have to count and calculate every step you take.

I've got another great story and then we'll move on to the next chapter.

Is it good to always have some money set aside? A friend in London, over a beer, said,

-One day, I got married. I love her as much today as I did then. But with the money we never got along. I some money from her, exactly 5000 euros, which I had set aside before the wedding, just in case of hard times. The money was fine and I didn't need it. One day, we got upset, I don't know what stupidity was there. To make peace with her, I went and bought her a professional photo camera, which I knew she wanted. After I came home with the gift and made her very happy, was not coming to believe what a wonderful gift she received and of course she asked the question. „Where did I get so much money, so suddenly?". That's all I had to do, I told her about the 5000 euros and exactly 4500 euros left. That was on a Monday. On Friday we had 0 euros left. As I told her about them, it took her a few hours in the evening to convince me to put new tiles and tile the bathroom and the kitchen, and other small improvements. Just so you know, how well the money was until she found out about...

CHAPTER 11

BUSINESS IDEAS

YOU PROBABLY WANT TO learn a secret or find a safe recipe for success. What I can tell you is this: dream, make a good plan and act! To be able to say you're alive, you have to live your dream. Have fun!

First, you need, one way or another, to reach learning, at that point where you have a clear vision of what you want to do. I am sure that, by this point, you have had several business ideas in your mind, which were then left behind because of fears, mistrust or lack of support from those around you. If, at the moment, you don't have anything clear in mind about what you can do, go back to those moments when you dreamed of creating something. Return to the passions of your childhood, to the pleasures you have experienced, to anything that brings you joy. That's where you have to start.

> *Choose a job you love, and you*
> *will never have to work a day in your life.*
>
> *Confucius*

Have you ever thought about making soaps, cakes, pottery, a museum house or something else? In any field, you can create a name, a brand. That's what it means to be ready to get started and that's what you can do by reading. You know a thing or few about yoga, you like it, you want to teach others and even earn money for your living, and then keep it a city-wide course? Read and learn about. After reading 20 books on yoga and practicing for a while, you will be able to consider yourself fit to give lessons. This was an example. In whichever field you choose to go, it takes a lot of work and knowledge. Then you have to have a positive mind.

Jesus says in the Bible:
For I assure you: If you have faith the size of a
mustard seed, you will tell this mountain,
'Move from here to there,' and it will move.
Nothing will be impossible for you.

Matthew 17: 20

You have to dream, you have to want to see yourself there where you want to go. If you can do that, you can already set yourself to fun. Your daily activity must be fun. Work without pleasure. Without fun doesn't make sense. If you end up having fun doing what you want to do, you gain confidence and no one will be able to tell you that you will not be successful. Because you already have success.

Let yourself be drawn by the stronger pull of
that which you truly love.

Rumi

A few days ago, I was in a friend house. In time we was talking in the living room, their little girl who is only a few years old, got on the piano chair and started playing a few random notes and it didn't sound bad at all. Her parents told me that they little girl wanted to play the piano and they sent her to take lessons. At the time, I thought some kids didn't have access to piano or other musical instruments.

Not ever seeing a piano, of course, you have no idea that you can play one or that would become the passion of your life. The moral is that if you don't know things, you don't want them. You don't know that there is juice in the coconut, you don't need juice of coconut. Simple. In business it's the same, if you don't know enough types of business, you might not find one you want to hit for your own. Search, learn, read, find and then choose.

Find your passion. If you want to be surrounded by nature, you can choose to develop a guesthouse or animal farm. If you want fun, you can open a club or paintball park.

I can give you some business ideas or ideas to find something to do and the choice is yours, but better try to find the domain you're bound to. Don't think that a business area that works for me will bring you joy or money. Besides, things change, life changes. You can't always choose what others choose. If you don't choose what suits you, you won't be able to love it and therefore you won't give and take enough. Even if there's a million hostels, a million farms, a million clubs, you do your business, your own way, in a new way. That's the key, not to go after others, but on the path of your soul.

If you don't know exactly how to translate your passion into a business, connect your passion to what people need or what they want to buy, don't just focus on what you want to sell. Be flexible. Serve people, search for information about people's needs, try to help and connect people's needs to your passion at the same time. Look for passion in everything you do, don't look for money. For example, you like sports, specifically field tennis. What do people need? Health, movement! Well, you can become a tennis coach. Learn, read and practice. Then look for funds and money to open your own tennis court. If you do this with passion, you will find people who appreciate you and choose this activity for movement, on your land. Out of passion for tennis, you will create competitions, online pages for marketing and so on.

Through perseverance many people win success out of what seemed destined to be certain failure.

Benjamin Disraeli

Jewelry
In my first book I wrote about my life and the experiences I went through. One of them – my first business – was the purchase and sale of silver

jewelry, then I construct them. I didn't know much about what it meant to have a company, but I learned what I had to do after ordering the first pack of jewelry from Thailand. After the package with 77 pieces of silver (rings, earrings and chains) arrived in Otopeni Airport, I was called by the customs agent, who asked me for my company's details and address. Because I didn't have a company yet and I just made a probation order, I decided it was time to start a serious business. I registered the company, I got the necessary notices from the Office of Consumer Protection (the most expensive), I registered as a jeweler sellers group and I received a certificate from them, I bought my cash register, I found an accountant, I bought an accounting software and so on. All of this seem a lot and expensive, but I solved all in less than 10 days, so that the package was not sent back to Thailand. Then I sold the pieces of silver in two days. Orders of thousands of pieces followed, some of them to be assembled. I recovered my money spent on paperwork and merchandise in less than a few weeks. It's worth it and it's easy, plus it's fun to create an occupation you like to earn money from. Then, in the summer, I was on a lake, with my feet in the water and the lights launched, knowing that somewhere in the world, someone was buying jewelry from me and I was cashing in every transaction from the third party seller. Even at night when I was sleeping, someone was selling jewelry for me. I wasn't making a lot of, but I was feeling free.

At the end of this chapter, I'll give you some business ideas, so, as examples, although you can find this on all the fences. It's better to find in your soul what you really want to do in your life. Until then, I'll tell you what I already know about the real estate business, because they're the place where you can invest from the beginning or after you have profits from another business.

For this year I made a list of plans and one of them was to buy 3 real estate. At the beginning of the year I didn't have any money set aside, I was really in debt. Now, summer hasn't come yet and I have the money for two. Another plan noted is to finish this book by the end of the year. It didn't come in the summer either, and here I am, keeping up with the plan.

Here are some lines and ideas related to the real estate business:

Do you have a house in the city and a yard big enough? Take money from the bank and build studio flats. Look for business partners. Double your money with them. How? Let me give you a valid example for Romania in smaller cities. Each partner puts 20,000 euros or more. You gather 6-7 people. You buy a 400-square-metre courtyard. Build as many studios as you can. Sell them. Count and see how much it gives you at the end. My calculation gives at least double the amount invested each of you after the win is split. Building studios, on land, in courtyards or gardens of houses in cities, is a very profitable business, as long as the law lets you build them. You can double your investment money, depending on the number of studios. An equally good deal is to rent them out.

In real estate, you have to have the cash. Even if you borrow money from the bank, you must already have it in your account. At first, you can't really negotiate on promises, that's where you need a lot of experience.

To gain from these businesses you have to buy at a good price. Even if that property is to be rented, you still have to buy it at a price at least 25% lower than that of the market. For that, you need cash money, at least a large part of it. If the price of that property falls during a financial crisis and you bought it during the peak period, by renting, you can keep your profit.

You can't know exactly what's going to happen to the economy, but you can control profits.

You need to know the value of a business or a real estate before you buy it. Don't try to guess. Chance is great to lose if you try to guess. You have to win on the purchase, because you don't know what will happen later. Thus, you have things under control in almost any situation.

Real estate is about negotiations. If you don't have the full amount, don't despair. Whoever has the money makes the rules of the game. Once, I wanted to buy a property, after the real estate agent posted an ad with that property at a price 15% lower than the market price. Do you know how much I bought the property? Less than 25% of the market price. How? I negotiated with the money on the table. When you have to take out a loan in the bank, it's harder to negotiate. When you put the money on the table, you run the game.

Once you get further into business, if you choose real estate, open an agency. Not for the work of the agency itself, but because people will come directly to you. You will have direct access to bargains, tenants and quick sales of your goods. You're going to spin them on your fingers. The real estate agency will support personal property and rents. In addition, you will also trade for others where you will get good commissions. The problem with the agency is this: you have to be there, permanently. It's one of those businesses that doesn't work without you. But it's for an early phase, and when you will raise enough money, you'll be able to give it up.

Another idea related to real estate is a „tenant's association". At the moment, tenants' associations are awfully unprofitable organizations for the owners attached to them. At least in small towns, they're a real mess. They charge, but they do very little for the zone that they're supposed to take care of. If you open a company like this, the investment might only be in a large office, employees, office equipment and furniture. Papers and marketing. You need a team of skilled people and a good legal adviser for a long-term work. A big deal, the size of a city. Smaller cities are the ideal places for this.

Then, by the way, all small towns are the ideal place for online business. Rents for storage spaces are greatly reduced. Employees work on lower wages. Your daily expenses are reduced. The walk between institutions takes short. You get to know people by name.

I was actually thinking for me, of proposing to others that can invest in a project together. There are many who have smaller amounts of money to start a business, but they are afraid of, or their money is not enough. Together we can afford the best accountant. We'll have the best plumber. We'll have a van together for transportation needs. We'll pay a cleaning company together. We'll pay the utility fees together. But most importantly, we're going to help each other. Every week, we'll have a business meeting, we'll talk about new ideas, new opportunities. We will pool all the knowledge acquired so far, advertise to each other (online and by any other means), enjoy in a good and legal way the relationships we have, each of us, at home or abroad.

With the money you spend anyway on commuting in a big city, you can have more comfort in a smaller city. For example, instead of commuting, you can pay a woman to take care of the house and iron your shirts for a few hours every few days. Together we can offer her a full-time job. Where you put that hours lost on the road will be used to your advantage. In a big city you seem to be living better, but the time wasted on the road, through the city, you're counting it? Money raised monthly, after expenses, how many are there? Or did you inherit a small fortune in a big city? Provide a good environment in a smaller city to develop with your own resources a dream business or a quiet life. Welcoming people would pave the way for you and help you in all of that. Or you can stay where you are and go to work for the rest of your life, so you can pay off your taxes and maintain what you already own.

I have a friend in London who in recent years has focused heavily on gymnastics and has almost become a personal fitness assistant. But she cannot afford to devote herself only to this pleasure. She have to go to work and school every day. On a weekend, we went out to talk and to have a drink. There, I had an idea. Namely, I proposed here to learn everything she can about this field, so that there are no more terms, movements, muscle groups and nutrition methods that she does not know. Then create in Romania a place for courses of a few days in this field, somewhere in the mountains. Even if the place is not owned by her, she can make a contract with one of the hotels that desperately need customers, so that she will not bother about the accommodation and meals of the clients, nor even the meal and accommodation for her. So here's another passion turned into business. It will even be able to sell CDs with films about fitness and nutrition, which will provide valuable information to those interested.

Be careful not to be discouraged on your way by those who gossip about those who earn money from passions. „You're doing this for money!" Well, even I, who earn from many places, if I want to devote much of my life to writing, I can't eat paper. Every person has needs, has a family and has his own problems to solve. You can't live off a passion as long as you don't make money from it. Lawyers don't show up for money? Footballers don't make money? Anyway, don't worry, let them talk!

Don't be afraid of failure! I was telling a friend that I'd rather focus for a year on raising funds to start a business, and then do my best to make it grow, than to work that year in a job that doesn't bring joy.

Think about the fact that the goal is not always money, but is the time spent in the way you want which is the biggest gain.

Look for assets that make money for you. Looking for businesses that bring in money without you being there all the time. The ultimate reason why the business has to go well is this: you have to buy assets!

You're not successful at the moment if you're not insured in the long term by money-making assets even when you're sleeping. Assets are of many kinds and it's very good to diversify. Not necessarily by the way of the asset, but by any means you can. If, from your company's profit, you buy apartments, try to buy in two cities, not in one. Look for the area to be very good and the price of the apartment as low as possible, in relation to the rent you will get from it. If you get your money back in less than 10 years from rent, the deal is a very good one.

Here are some other business ideas, but remember, even if they already exist almost everywhere, you have to do them in a different and authentic way (some of them with the help of European funds, if you want to do them in Europe):

– Anything related to the ecological field, „green" businesses. Examples: eco cosmetic products, paper

135

and plastic recycling, organic food, organic building materials;

– Craft activities, production of various traditional objects;

– Catering company;

– Paulownia plantation for furniture and timber manufacture;

– Mushroom cultivation;

– Hostel;

– Home for elderly;

– Website for those looking for a job (existing websites are made for those looking for employees, I mean that companies are posted to the majority, and my idea is to post potential employees to choose from, not the other way around);

– Sale of solar panels and mini wind turbines;

– Company of exterior insulation for houses;

– Internet and cable TV services in rural areas;

– Nutritional supplements store;

– Successful business in mountain areas: rental of bicycles, ATVs, sleds, adventure park;

– Nut plantation or fruit tree orchard;

– Rural revival in any way;

– Ornamental trees and shrubs;

– Cultivation of hemp;

– Beekeeping;

– Hen farm;

– Berries;

– A country hall for events in the vicinity of a city (look for a special place in nature);

– Private nursery school;

– Fish farm;

– Spring water bottling line;

– Flower greenhouse;

– Wine-growing plantation;

– Grain warehouse;

– Grain mill;

– Manufactures of metal profiles;

– Services in rural areas;

– Car repair shop;

– Knitwear and garments;

– Handmade jewelry;

– Transport and storage;

– Naturist clinic;

– Bakery;

– Rental of decorations;

– A good business idea is to create a place for people to come to nature for relaxation. A place away from noise, a green and warm place where people can come to heal their body and soul.

You can do a long-lasting business with passionate and trained people. Even if you haven't started, there's nothing to stop you from sharing your ideas coming from passion, with people on the same wavelength or looking for what you can offer. You might be surrounded by a great team, just by looking for it. If you don't try, you'll never know. As an example, if you want to develop an agro-tourism business in the mountains, invite a ski enthusiast in the winter season to offer ski lessons to tourists. Maybe it's his dream and he didn't know how to start. Behold, you give him this opportunity (reread the chapter *Values, models and relationships*). What prevents you from inviting someone who loves children, to do child-specific activities during summer periods? What stops you from doing whatever you want and with whom you want? Together with passionate people you can build a long-lasting and healthy business. And, why not, you get into other people's business. Don't forget to read a lot, don't forget the plan, to find a suitable name for your business and a representative logo.

CHAPTER 12

ACT

THE WHOLE WORLD IS YOURS. How you create it, that's how you see it, that's how you get it! What better to do than live your dream? Your dream is waiting for you to open your eyes and to live it!

Before you start, you need to know that everyone who has achieved something great in life, has worked for their soul and the joy of their team. And those who didn't, watched to the people they worked for, achieved something great.

Once you've chosen an area where you want to act, you need a very serious plan. Even if no one guarantees that you will stick to this plan or change it in the meantime, you still need to outline a plan. When you start on a road on the car, you look first for a route as easy as possible, or even two in case something unexpected occurs. Before you leave, you have to fill the tank with fuel, load the windshield washer can, check the car documents and make many other preparations. In business you have to do the same. You can't hit the road without knowing where you want to go, which direction you're going to go in, where you're going to sleep in the night on the road and so on.

Go to the ant, you sluggard; consider its ways and be wise!It has no commander, no overseer or ruler,yet it stores its provisions in summerand gathers its food at harvest.

How long will you lie there, you sluggard? When will you get up from your sleep? A little sleep, a little slumber, a little folding of the hands to rest— and poverty will come on you like a thief and scarcity like an armed man.

Proverbs 6: 6-11

The following steps are extremely important:

- Choose a domain you like;
- Think positively;
- Be disciplined;
- Set clear targets, however large, just put them on paper;
- Learn everything you can about your chosen field;
- Look for opportunities;
- Surround yourself with good people and give up those who drag you down;
- Overcome fears;
- Act;
- Finish what you have started.

I know people who, after years and years of training in a chosen field, besides work, have not taken up anything on their own. They did nothing but learn about the desired field. But they keep going to work every day and they're probably afraid to take the step. Sometimes happens that, if you don't do something in the now, you'll never do it. You will remain like those who, although they learn a lot, will never apply what they have learned.

If, in a group of people, I pick up a $100 bill and I ask "- Who gives me 50$ for it?" surely some people will wonder if I'm joking, and others will wonder if what I'm doing is real. Others will tell themselves it's a joke, but someone will take out 50 $ and will buy from me a hundred, thus doubling his money. That's the action in business. Business involves exchanges. Whether we're talking about apartments, land or objects. Whoever seeks and finds opportunities, while being open and determined, will certainly have much to gain. Sometimes I encounter opportunities like example with money in real estate. Some wondered if it was a joke, at which point they missed the start. The action makes a difference. You don't have to look to the top of the mountain if you don't dare to take the first step.

You've certainly heard these words:
„I'm going to sports tomorrow."
„I'm going to lose weight tomorrow."
„I'll start learning tomorrow."
„I'll start reading tomorrow."
„I'm going to quit smoking tomorrow."
„I'll give up drinking tomorrow."
By procrastination, your plan can go to the fore. And, don't forget, the gated moment doesn't exist. There's only „now."

Here's an example of how money comes at money. Action, to action. The more you do for yourself and for your dream, the more you attract of what you do. A few days ago, I received an e-mail from one of the best-known online book-selling platforms. In the e-mail I was told that: „The more sales you have, the more you get on top, and they offer some super cash prizes to those in the top 100". That means the more you do, the more you sell, the more you invest, the more they all come to you, in what you do. Hence the word „money comes to money". If you get to work and invest passion and love in what you do, they all come back, much more."

Whatever you have chosen or you will choose to do, it takes time, or it really doesn't have an ending. The action is followed by effects, but it depends on the chosen field. BE PATIENT! Not all come at once, good or bad. Imagine what it would be like to have all your pimples on your face in the same time?

Our greatest glory is not in never falling, but in rising every time we fall
Confucius

When I was a kid, I had a cat I loved very much. I could write a lot about her, we had a lot of adventures together. I passed it several times to the „obituary page", so that after a few days, the poor of it, to appear home again. I also saw the fur crushed by the asphalt run over by the cars, and then it turned out to be the fur of another cat. Until one day, coming home, after a weekend away, I found the cat bitten on the head by who knows what animal, horribly infected. After much crying, ours and the cat, after nothing could be done and her condition worsened, because was unable to eat, my mother decided to kill her. My mother, who didn't kill a fly. We heard the cat crying at night and we couldn't sleep. Often I was crying too, sitting next to the cat and petting her. She was lying under the kitchen stove, she couldn't get up. She had half of her head an infected wound, she couldn't eat and was just making some sounds, like a cry, breaking my heart. There was enormous suffering in the house, around the cat. One day, we went to the bridge at Mureş River, with the cat in my arms and in the trunk of the car with a plastic bag and a brick ready for it. To this day I don't know what happened to my mother who took me to see something like this, because it was the only experience of this nature that I saw and heard of in my family, but it was kind of a mutual decision. Seeing the cat in the bag by the brick, my uncle, also present, broke down in tears. I was shaking. My mom couldn't throw the bag. We got in the car to go back home, but mom remembered the suffering especially of the cat. She got out of the car again and threw the net off the bridge, directly in Mureş, with the cat and everything. I jumped out of the car and got to see the net, which didn't sink directly. Because of some air inside, it took some time to get out through the specially made little holes. My screams followed, tears and crying, for days. The next mornings, when I woke up, I was waiting for the cat to come to my bed, and then, after a few moments, I remembered again that it was gone and I was crying to break my heart again and again. After all these nights of torment of the cat, I felt her still struggling somewhere. But I wasn't mad at my mom, I understood that her decision was the best.

About a week later, while I was washing my hands in the bathroom, I heard my mother, from the kitchen, talking to me:

-Guess who came home! Guess! You guessed!

The cat had a dry head wound, some kind of peel from that wound. How she got out of there I don't know, what an energy shock she might have caught, but if you don't take my word for it that this really happened, then close this book and throw it in fire! Weeks of play and fun followed, until I locked the cat in a closet of a public institution and forgot here there. About a Thursday. On Sunday morning I was looking at Tom & Jerry cartoons on the TV and my mom says, „Didn't you see the cat? She's been missing for a few days!" We jumped out of bed like a real warriors, starting together to save the princess. We couldn't find here there, but later finding out that the cleaning lady was about having a heart attack because of the noises in the empty building on

Saturday morning. The princess arrived home somewhere on Monday or Tuesday, safely.

If we're talking about action and the right time, remember my cat, there, in her bag on the river, in the mouth of death. With all the powers gathered, the action made the difference between life and death. Action also makes the difference between success and failure. Of course, you can also act in the wrong direction when you don't know what you're doing, but the failure is at home when all your plans are missing the action.

Through action you learn. Facing challenges, you learn better to know what you want and what you can, you know your powers, I know others better and you see who you are.

Business action can be similar to watering a flower, but it takes physical and intellectual work. Continuous learning requires a lot of your energy. You might think you know about sales, knowing that you learned about it 10 years ago. But what you've learned in the past may no longer be valid or useful today. The principles are the same, but the methods have changed. You need to get up to speed on what's new. It's no use of talking if you don't know how to turn on a computer in the 21st century. You have to take action on all fronts.

Don't let this day go by for nothing.

In sales of any kind, you need a market. Besides online, you have a list of friends and acquaintances. You may never have thought of that, but you know so many people. From the lady at the bakery or your doctor, to friends of your school classmates. Depends on what you sell, but the big circle of acquaintances might be going to help you enormously. If you don't have these people on a social media page on the internet, put all these names on a piece of paper and you'll be amazed at how many people you know. It's also a starting point in some businesses.

Focus on marketing and network. You'll need publicity. Start by learning about what it means and learn as many ways as you can to make your business or product known.

Related to advertising and promotion, look to do something new, unique. If you sell roses, make a special bow, yours, to be caught by every rose. Do something to be known for, to stand out. The moment you advertise your product, you'll come in front of people with something unique. This gives you the chance to be promoted better and people with influence in the media take part in supporting your product. If you come up with something you've seen before, it's not really of any interest to anyone, unless you promote your product in an aggressive manner, which generally costs a lot. There's no negative publicity, just advertising. However, take care of the image of your product.

Then think about little advertising tricks that can help others too. For example, you can collaborate with a café bar. There, every person who buys a coffee can receive a flyer containing a discount code for your product. This way you find customers through free advertising, the discount being one you can afford. The owner of the café bar also wins, offering, in addition to coffee, a promotional code. This will make happier his customers. Think...

Have you ever ridded a bike? If so, you remember that the first time you did it came out some kind of dramatic comedy. But ambition made you learn. Once you find your balance and realize you can, it's like you're not going to stop pedaling. That's kind of the way to your dream. Once you find your balance and see that it can, you become unstoppable. Act!

A lot of people who don't make big things, they're looking for excuses. They always find justifications for failure, for lack of action, for laziness. Successful people are looking for solutions. We all love comfort and safety, but them will come as an effect of our creation.

Nothing is worth more than this day.
Goethe

Today's life, if you allow it, invades your life more than it did in the past. Everything moves much faster, there are unlimited options and opportunities in number, remote communication is done instantly. That's not bad at all, because it gives you the opportunity to make choices. Today, on a day off, you can visit someone in another city, go back to yours for shopping and, in a few hours, be in a place to spend your weekend. At the same time, you can communicate with friends and family elsewhere, you can solve work problems. You can do so much in such a short time. If you act...

There are a thousand excuses for failure,
but never a good reason.

Mark Twain

So work and learn, to be good at what you do and do the best you can, where you are, with what you have. Use the time you've been given! Don't just be a spectator, don't make excuses, but send all your energy to create your dream life!

ANDY HERTZ

<u>EPILOGUE</u>

As soon as you trust yourself,
you will know how to live.

Goethe

FOR FEARS TO KEEP YOU AWAY from your dream, away from your purpose, away from your purpose, I find life wasting. Do you know how? It's like getting an hour of life and a mountain in front of you. So. Otherwise, nothing. Then, if you go up or not, the time you've been given will pass anyway. And you either stay put or you go around in a circle, and you say that something might happen to you on the way up, or, you go up and you

151

go up, and you go up, and you go up, and you go up, and you become unstoppable.

Decades from now, I wish you to look in the mirror and say to yourself, „-Good thing I didn't give up. Today I could have been a loser, I could have looked and found reasons for failure. But I didn't. I would not want to meet today, in the mirror, the person who I could have remained, but I look straight in the eye, the person who I became through my own powers. That's me!"

Don't turn into a parent forgetting your passions, don't turn into an obsessive passion, don't forget that you have a family and don't turn into a passion forgetting friends, sports, hobbies. Enjoy diversity. Be grateful for what you have received, for your body, for your mind, for what you can do, for your health. Then try to change the world for the better and discover your success.

Success can mean anything, everyone perceives it in a different way. For one it means money or career fulfillment, for another, peace of mind or winning a competition. I say success is a combination of success from many plans. Career, family, peace of mind, health and so on. But while each of us is born with various shortcomings, the challenge is to cover them with skills received with birth. So instead of creating problems, solve problems. You can't achieve success by creating problems every step of the way or finding reasons for failure. They can be found everywhere, as well as the reasons for success.

Be the change you wish to see in the world.

Mahatma Gandhi

Imagine a moment when you pour all your anger on a person, and she or he puts a mirror between. The frame disappears and it's just you, with you. Screaming. Pouring poison. Spitting venom.

Imagine a moment when you let a wave of your love flow on a person, and she or he puts a mirror between. The frame disappears and it's just you, with you. Loving. Pouring light. Looking at those warm eyes in peace and quiet.

The life you lead is due to you. For this reason, you need to set your mind in such a way that you can lead yourself to abundance, success or whatever you want. But you don't have to make sudden moves! Dance, play, learn, float, descend to the earth, fly, discover, make smooth movements, thus become a better and more beautiful human being. Send beautiful thoughts to the people and the sky will light up for you. A better world means better people.

Until you accept what you have already received from life, namely your body, your family, your past, until then you will not be able to accept or find what part of the outside is: people, future, success... Love yourself, then, others will love you. The walls will fall and you will find freedom!

Don't accept circumstances that don't make you happy!

-Let him see! or -She'll be sorry!

I've heard this words at some people, after a breakup: „-She/he will see what it's like without me!" Don't do that! Especially in business. Either you save the business (or the relationship) or you let it go. Don't waste your energy unnecessarily. So many people cling to people from the past or to the wrong jobs, and this happens because of the ego. I was saying above, dance, play, live. Life passes, you don't have time for vanity. In fact, you don't have time for a lot of things you keep doing. If you sometimes spend time in silence and meditation, you would be able to discover these things. It's very important to understand the things, the places and the people you have to give up. To find the exit from the tunnel, you must first find the light. You have to find the point, the meaning...

Because I have reached the end of this book and because I have not really talked about retirement, which is a suitable topic for anyone, in short, I do not think the best option is to raise your pension by paying a monthly amount of money. The pension is made through well-made investments. Keep your money under control. And, remember, the pension doesn't have to come as a release. Retirement must not become a target, a goal. That would actually be a sadness if that were to happen. Ideally, you should prepare some good investments for that period, then work as much as you want and as much as you can, in your chosen field, with passion. When it's time for rest, the money will come from what you've built.

Wherever you are on your way, invest in yourself further, the road has not come to an end. Educating yourself as a manager of your own life never ends. Times change, you can't fall behind. A man who worked in sales 10 years ago, who thinks he knows everything, is actually out of. The technology and the internet have developed so much that he doesn't even know how much he's overlooked. You must always read new books, go to a course or seminar. You're going to agree with me.

You don't have to be a champion in astronomy, but if you stop at arithmetic, at additions, you stay in the kindergarten of mathematics. You don't have to be a sports champion, but if you stop after five crunches, it is very bad. You don't have to be a money-making champion, but if the money doesn't come from what you like to do, you're going with them to buy things that you don't need. The

155

unfortunate spend more money on useless things. You don't have to be a champion friend, but to have good people around you, it's your choice. You don't have to be a champion in love, but if you don't love, you live for nothing. I would give you happiness wrapped in gifts and wealth, but that's not possible. You must follow the path of your soul...

Choose to do things with love for others. If you plant a tree without love, at least do it as best you can. The tree will hold shadow for others in summer, it will bear fruits and it will exist because of you. If you plant a tree and, with it, you plant a piece of your soul there, it'll be yours, a part of yours. It will give you the same fruits, but they will taste sweeter. Because you will wait for them, you will keep the seeds of the fruit and plant them carefully. You would even gather the dried leaves to adorn your hair or house with them. It would be a story, the story from your garden, your orchard, your colorful world. Seek to do things with love, so they will grow and you will grow with them. You'll fill the world with beautiful stories.

Life sometimes is very hard, but it's worth every minute. You don't live yesterday, you don't live tomorrow. The only time you live is now. Live beautifully and become better, become free, become what you want to be!

Keep calm and make sure you can do whatever you want. Whatever you think can come true. Life is too short to expect changes from the outside.

You were born to win, not to feel sorry for yourself!

ANDY HERTZ

THE END

ANDY HERTZ

www.ingramcontent.com/pod-product-compliance
Lightning Source LLC
Chambersburg PA
CBHW030640220526
45463CB00004B/1595